Life with God

Life with God

by

Mike and Michele Green

Bless God Publishing
Gainesville, FL 32602 USA

Bless God Publishing
Gainesville, FL 32602 USA

Life With God
by Mike and Michele Green

Copyright ©2007 by Bless God Publishing

All rights reserved. Under International Copyright Law, no part of this publication may be reproduced, stored, or transmitted by any means—electronic, mechanical, photographic (photocopy), recording, or otherwise—without written permission from the Publisher.

Printed in the United States of America.

Library of Congress Catalog Card Number: pending
International Standard Book Number: 978-0-615-16801-2

Scripture quotations in this book are taken from the *Holy Bible, New International Version*®. NIV®. Copyright © 1973, 1978, 1984 by International Bible Society. Used by permission of Zondervan. All rights reserved.

Contents

Introduction vii
The Light Shines 1
The Cost of Commitment 11
Closing the Door. 17
Suffering in Perspective 23
God Rents the Truck. 27
Formulas or Faith? 35
God Still Heals 41
God and the Tax Man. 51
Honey and Powdered Milk 57
God, the Auto Mechanic. 61
The Tale of Two Fifties 67
God Pays the Rent. 75
Miraculous Tuition 81
Confusing the Priorities. 89
More Than Enough. 95
Epilogue 103

Short Stories by Mike Green

The Christmas Vision 107
The Tree and the Bird 117
The Man, the Mountain and God. 125
The Silver Cup 133
Further Understanding of Life With God 147
Prayer 153

Introduction

This book is a collection of stories. The stories are progressive in that they are written in the order they occurred. In them we share some of the wonderful and, sometimes miraculous, events that have taken place in our life as we have endeavored to know God personally. The stories are true, they happened just as we report them. We did not embellish the details, nor do we want to interpret the events, or argue for their validity. Our hope is that by relating the events as they happened we might help the reader better understand the personal nature of God. For us, He is a loving Father who desires to rescue, heal, restore, and bless all of His creation. Yet to experience His love we must know Him. To know Him we must spend time with Him. We do this primarily by reading His Word, the Bible. We can also pursue a personal relationship with Him, learning to hear His voice and to follow His guidance. Over the past twenty or so years we have learned a simple but certainly life-changing truth. That is: As we pursue Him, He will reveal Himself to us.

As you read we would caution you to remember this: The beginning of a proper understanding of God is a result of believing what He says about Himself in the Bible. However, understanding the mystery of God's eternal nature is a spiritual endeavor, not an intellectual one. The corrupt and finite human intellect will never uncover the majesty of God simply by studying. God's unique and glorious divine nature is unlike anything man can conceive and thus He cannot be known intellectually. A true and right understanding of God can only be accomplished with the assistance of His Holy Spirit. He is the teacher through whom we learn to know God. We have access to His Spirit only through our personal commitment to enthrone Jesus Christ as the lord of our life.

Our fervent prayer is that by reading our book you will desire to know Him even better than you know Him now. And if you do not know Him personally now, we pray He will reveal Himself to you that you may learn to trust Him, love Him, and enjoy Him throughout the endless days of your life.

Mike and Michele Green
St. Augustine, Florida
2007

Chapter 1

The Light Shines

*I am the way, the truth, and the light.
No one comes to the Father except through me
(John 14:6).*

I was 16 years old. High School was not going well. I was confused about a lot of things. Those things were the major issues one encounters as a teenager. Things like identity, love, school, and the future. I sought the counsel of many adults. But the wisdom they offered didn't seem to touch the nagging uncertainty that had become my constant companion. At work, my boss told me to get a good job, make a lot of money, and retire early. It was and still is good advice. But at the time I didn't know how one could make a lot of money, surfing! At school, the guidance counselor implied that I wasn't really college material and suggested I might consider the military. But at the time, the United States was engaged in a controversial war in Southeast Asia. Many of this country's youngest and brightest men were killing and being killed over there. I wasn't very patriotic and lacked the courage required to commit murder or die for a cause I didn't understand. My parents were busy working to provide for the six of us kids. Neither of them had much to say about college or life in general. They spent most of their time trying to stay ahead of the weekly grocery bill.

All of these well meaning people wanted to help but they couldn't. They didn't have what I needed. It wasn't their fault. I didn't know what I wanted. It was a very difficult time.

One night, after work, I drove to the beach. I just wanted to sit quietly and ponder the confusing maze that was my life. I went to my favorite spot. It was secluded and I was sure I wouldn't be bothered by intruders. I took my seat at the foot of the coconut palm tree. Leaning back, I inhaled a deep exhilarating lung full of the salt-laden sea air. The sky was filled with millions of stars. The easterly breeze carried the scent of the ocean mingled with the pungent aroma of sea grapes and drying Sargasso weed. The surf was rustling its familiar tune and the breaking waves laid their phosphorescent trails in crisscrossing rows along the sandy beach.

I loved the beach, and still do, since the first time I saw it as a five year old. And I especially enjoyed it at night. It was my friend and always welcomed me regardless of my mood. I could always be me, confused and vulnerable, without fear of rebuke. I went there often to be alone and to think through things. But on that particular night, as I sat there drinking in the familiar scene, I noticed something new and different. I couldn't describe it but I knew something was different about this night. I studied the sea, looking for clues. I closed my eyes and felt the breeze caress my face. I inhaled the fragrance of the seashore. I listened as the palm tree whispered its song to the rhythm of the breaking surf rustling it's way across the sandbar. Finally, tilting my head heavenward I opened my eyes and gazed into the star-sprinkled night sky.

It was as I studied the cosmic display that I began to touch what I was feeling. It was new and fresh and charged my body and soul with electricity, while at the same time filling me with a peace I had never before felt. It was as if God was speaking directly to me. I hadn't asked Him to speak to me. At the time I didn't claim to know Him or even much about Him. Yet, though His voice was inaudible I couldn't ignore it. As I listened I heard Him say, "I'm here and I want you to know me." It was simple and profound. There was no doubt I heard it plainly. I struggled to comprehend and accept the peace I was experiencing. I was alone, on the beach, there wasn't a human being in sight, and yet I felt like I was in the presence of someone very important. I was both at peace, and embarrassingly self-conscious. I wanted to stay there forever savoring the moment, and yet at the same time, I wanted to run away and hide.

With my eyes riveted on the sky I managed to speak. I addressed His awesome presence respectfully, "I know you're there, and that you want me to know you." And then I added, with more conviction than a trembling insecure sixteen-year-old can possess, "I'll do whatever it takes to find you."

That night on the beach was very significant for me. As I reflect on it years later I see it was the turning point in my life. It marked the beginning of my search for a personal relationship with God. For the next twenty years I studied numerous religious philosophies in an attempt to fulfill the burning desire of my heart, to know God personally. My quest was fueled by the moral and social changes that exploded within American society during the 1960s. The hunger for personal change within me was given the go ahead by the political unrest and moral decline of the period.

Children were rebelling against the mediocre religious mores of their parents. "Why adhere to a religious dogma if it didn't improve the quality of life?" they asked. White Anglo Saxon Protestantism was being challenged from every side. First, African Americans wanted their civil rights. Next women wanted to be liberated from their traditional back seat role in society. Then, Native Americans wanted their land back, young people wanted freedom from the tyranny of the adult double standard. The new battle cry for an entire generation became "tune in, turn on, and drop out." Bob Dylan mumbled, "The time's they are a-changin" and the Beatles sang, "All you need is love." And I believed both of them.

The irony of that period of my life was, for all the mind altering drugs I ingested, and all the metaphysical books I read, I didn't feel any closer to God. I ate LSD like it was candy, read East Indian religious books, practiced several different forms of yoga, became a vegetarian, and fasted and meditated. Even though my mind had been "expanded" and I was physically very healthy, I did not know God. And I could not honestly ignore the facts. Frustrated by the emptiness I found in one belief system, I tried another, and then another. I tried many different avenues on the road to enlightenment over a period of twenty years.

During that time I met many others like myself, who wanted to know God personally. But they drifted into and out of my life. One, however, stayed. Her name was Michele, and she became my wife. We then pursued our study of God together.

Eventually, Michele and I settled into transcendental meditation. TM's guru leader, Maharisi Mahesh Yogi, claimed his method would lead the devotee to enlightenment, or God consciousness, in one lifetime. But after eight years of faithfully following his regimen, including taking advanced courses costing many thousands of dollars, I was no closer to God.

It was then that a favorite line of Maharishi's struck me. "If what you are doing gets results, why question it?" He talked about how the honey bee flies from flower to flower extracting all the nectar from each one as he goes. He reasoned smugly that if the bumblebee ever landed on a flower with an inexhaustible supply of nectar, he would never fly again. For me, TM had not proved to be a flower flowing with unending nectar. What I had been doing for eight years had not delivered the goods. I was getting anxious to fly on to another flower.

During that time I had become involved in business and was working many long hours building a thriving business and an honorable reputation among my workaholic peers. To help TM relieve the stress of my lifestyle I began drinking alcohol again.

Drinking had always been a big part of my family of origin's daily routine. My father lived on beer. And my older brother and sister started drinking while in high school. I followed their lead by the time I was fourteen. During the "enlightened" years I had sworn off the stuff. It was during that same time that I had given up drugs. But to deal with the pressure of business and work I resumed my relationship with beer. Soon though beer was not enough to take the edge off. So, I began drinking rum. It provided a quicker trip to "the land without the edge," I reasoned, so it was more cost effective.

For the next several years I developed a dangerous drinking habit. The routine went like this. Beer from lunch through "quittin' time." Then rum and tonic from quittin' time to bedtime. The business continued to grow. The pressure continued to build. And the rum continued to flow. Time and again I pledged to my wife I would quit drinking, but sadly, I knew I couldn't.

After one particular night of hard drinking, I was left alone in my hotel room in down town Dallas. I had been entertaining some gentlemen from a sales company and had consumed a lethal quantity of margaritas. After the bartender asked us to leave so he could close up, I rode the elevator to my room. I was alone. The party was over.

As I stood staring out of the window of my fourteenth floor room, I was overwhelmed by how far I had come in my search for God. It felt like I had come full circle. From the innocent beginning of my quest during my high school years, through the metaphysics and drugs of the sixties, the Hinduism of the seventies and the TM of the early eighties, there I was, drunk again! What had happened? I had been looking for God. Was this the end of all that searching? Could the truth be, there was no God?

As I leaned against the cool glass of the window staring out on the Dallas skyline I remembered the night on the beach when I first felt God's presence. Then, leaning against that window, for a second or two, I felt His presence again. This time it was almost imperceptible, but I felt it. He didn't speak this time, or if He did I was too drunk to hear Him. But I knew He was with me. As I had done in the first encounter, I chose to speak again. "God, I have been looking for you since I was sixteen, and I feel like I'm further away from you now than I was then." I caught my breath and continued, "All I have ever wanted was to know you, like I believe you want me to. And I have tried. But I've blown it. And I'm not going to try anymore. I just don't have any energy left to keep looking. If you want me to know you, you're going to have to do something about it, because I can't."

The Light Shines

When I returned home from my trip to Dallas nothing changed. My wife was glad to see me and I was happy to be with her and our fourteen-month-old daughter again. I didn't know it but God was at work in my life as never before.

Throughout the years of building the business it had become my custom to sit in front of the television and drink myself to sleep. I usually channel surfed unless boxing was on ESPN. My wife hated boxing and would not join me on the couch as I watched. I would sit there flinching with every punch that landed as two modern gladiators tried to get as close to killing each other as was legally possible. Sometimes they succeeded. Why were we outraged when one occasionally died of a brain hemorrhage?

As I watched boxing I would surf the channels during the one-minute break between rounds. After my Dallas encounter with God I began to be attracted to a TV evangelist. I would stop at his channel to hear what the narrow-minded guy had to say. I'm not sure what attracted me at first. It may have been the taped testimonies people shared. I gazed slack jawed as normal people like me talked about how God miraculously saved them from death, or divorce, or financial ruin. Night after night I watched. But I only watched for a minute, between rounds. My wife thought it was just as strange for me to watch the religious show, as it was to watch boxing!

The more I watched, the more impressed I was by the man on religious TV. Within a month I was staying up late to see the whole show from beginning to end. Pat Robertson and the 700 Club became my favorite show on TV. I watched it in the morning during the live broadcast. Then I watched it twice at night. Once at six PM on one channel, and again at 10 PM on another channel. Pretty soon I was watching Sunday morning TV. And religious programs were the only shows on!

One day I prayed with the man on TV. I thought to myself, "This is kind of silly but what could it hurt?" I prayed to receive Jesus as my Lord and Savior. But nothing about me changed.

A month or so later I prayed again, and still nothing changed.

Then one day as I was watching the 700 Club Ben Kenchlow said, "Don't turn off your TV. You know you have looked everywhere for a relationship with God. And nothing you have tried has worked. But today, if you'll pray with me I believe God will reveal Himself to you. You know it doesn't matter how much material stuff you have, if you don't have Jesus Christ as Lord of your life, you don't have anything." And he prayed and I prayed after him. And when he was finished praying he said, "Now do yourself a favor. It is very important that you tell someone what you've just done. So, pick up your phone and call the number on the TV screen. Tell someone that you just prayed to surrender your life to the Lordship of Jesus Christ."

I turned to the phone, picked it up and dialed. When the woman answered and asked, "How can I help you?" I began, "I just" and my throat locked up. So I tried again, "I just ... uh ... pr ... pray ... pray-eed," I stammered, "with the man on TV and ... and ... I uh ... accepted ... Je ... Je ..." and as I fought to get the word "Jesus," out I felt an emotional dam was about to explode. I tried again" I just accepted, Jesus, as ... ma ... my ... Lord ... and ... Savior." And when I said "savior," I felt as if my heart would shatter into a million pieces! There was a tearing inside my chest and a strange heat filled my throat and neck. My eyes filled with tears and as the dam broke I began to cry uncontrollably! I felt embarrassed as the woman on the phone began to praise God for my salvation. She was praising God and I was crying like a baby.

I was embarrassed but for some reason it felt real good to cry uncontrollably. As I continued to cry I knew without a shadow of doubt I had discovered something very special. I thought, "Can this really be happening to me?"

As I collected myself and tried to settle down I knew something strangely wonderful had happened to me. Somehow, as weird as it was, I knew in my heart, I had met God personally.

A week or so later, Michele, also accepted Jesus as her Lord and Savior. The 700 Club sent us some information describing what had happened to us. They encouraged us to get a Bible we could understand and start reading it. They said we also needed to develop a prayer life. They called it talking to God, our Heavenly Father, because He wanted to hear from us. So we bought several different translations of the Bible. Prior to that I did not know there was more than one translation. We bought the New American Standard Bible, The Living Bible, The New International Version, and one from the 700 Club called, The Book. We would sit on the couch in the evenings and read for hours. Then we would pray just like we were told to do. Every day was filled with revelation upon glorious revelation as the Holy Spirit disclosed to us the mysteries of God. And God changed our lives! We were overjoyed to know we knew God, that He was real, and that He wanted us to know Him personally. Our life has never been the same!

Chapter 2

The Cost of Commitment

Let not your heart be troubled; you believe in God, believe also in me (John 14:1).

I was one of them now! Those peculiar people I had quietly mocked for their conservative narrow-minded thinking. I was a born again Christian. I wasn't sure what a born again Christian was, but I knew I was one of them. At least that's what the literature sent to me by the 700 Club said. I had been born again from above, by the Spirit of God! It was pretty amazing. During the first week after my crying fit on the phone, I became increasingly aware that I didn't need TM anymore. I had a peace way down deep inside of me that I had not known before. Michele wasn't sure what had happened. All she knew was that I watched a lot of Christian television programs. She even made comments like, "Why are you watching that stuff?"

One day when she asked me if I wanted to do my TM program with her, as had been our daily routine for eight years, I said "No." I knew the answer made her nervous but

I didn't know what else to say. She pushed the issue and I responded very calmly, "I'm not going to do TM anymore."

"What, are you talking about?" she asked.

"Well, uh, you know those guys on TV? Those Christians?" I offered cautiously. Agitated she said, "Yes, the ones you have been watching for months?"

"Well, I'm one of them." It sounded so weak, but it was all I could manage in the way of an explanation. "I'm a born again Christian, and I'm not going to do TM anymore." My words hung suspended in mid air. I was perfectly calm and I knew she was really confused. She turned around speechless and marched out of the house, got in the car and drove off down the street.

When she came home she was calm and collected. We didn't speak of my confession again that day. But the next weekend while we were watching the 700 Club together, she prayed with the man on TV and I prayed with her. And she caught the same wonderful disease I had!

The next year of our life was filled with amazing grace. We were in love with God. He felt so close, so real, so alive. We bought three or four translations of the Bible and read for hours. We met a wonderful older couple from a nearby city and they introduced us to the spirit-filled life. And if our new life in Christ was good before receiving the Baptism of the Spirit, afterward it was incredible! We marveled as God began to use us to help other people understand and receive His love.

In general, our new life with God was wonderful. But there was one aspect our life that wasn't so pleasant. Shortly after our conversion experience, Michele and I developed

The Cost of Commitment

physical symptoms similar to a bad cold or flu. We both suffered from fevers, coughing, diarrhea, and vomiting. We lost our ability to hold food down so we lost a lot of weight and had to be very careful what we ate. At first we did not see any connection between our new life with God and our sickness.

In the midst of our suffering the most difficult thing was to watch our beautiful baby daughter writhe in pain during the night as she slept. She was only eighteen months old when we surrendered our lives to the Lordship of Christ. She was typically a good baby who ate anything we put in front of her. Amazingly, she started sleeping through the night two or three months after she was born. But after we surrendered our lives to God, her sleep became disturbed. On more than one occasion she reported seeing evil looking entities in her room. Since she didn't watch TV where she may have seen something like that and she wasn't given to exaggeration, we became very concerned. That's when we started to learn about demons.

Through our Bible reading we came to understand that demons were a part of God's created order. We weren't sure why God allowed them to operate but we saw that Jesus dealt with them quite often. We were amazed that the first time he preached in the synagogue after his baptism by John the Baptist, a demon spoke through a member of the congregation! Our Bible study revealed they were messengers of satan sent to harass and oppress mankind. They appeared to have two basic goals. First, they tried to keep people from believing the truth about Jesus and second, they tried to keep people who believed the truth about Jesus, from living like Jesus.

During that time we met several people who knew more than we did about demons and they came to our home and prayed for us. They said the Holy Spirit showed them that the demons wanted to stop us from doing what God wanted us to do. It was a scary thought but it seemed to be a reasonable explanation of our symptoms. And as I thought about it some more I came to believe that demons were very busy in my life from the time I heard God on the beach until the time I prayed with Ben Kenchlow!

The demonic attack continued relentlessly throughout the first year of our life with God. For twelve months there was not a week when all three of us were healthy. Either one or more of us was sick for a year! My wife's cough became so severe that she separated two ribs. Sores covered our tongues making it impossible to speak without pain. The stomach ailments we suffered made eating futile.

Our daughter's sleep became increasingly fitful. She would waken in the night screaming in pain. Night after night I would go to her room and take her in my arms and pray for her. She was so distressed that she would writhe and twist in my arms as if she was trying to get away from something frightening. As I prayed for her the fear would subside and she would eventually fall asleep. Sometimes as I placed her gently back in her bed she would wake up and start the painful routine all over again. There were some nights when neither of us slept more than a couple hours, fifteen or twenty minute at a time. It was exhausting!

The end of this madness happened rather dramatically late one night near the end of the twelfth month. I was walking back and forth in the living room praying for Lindsey while Michele sat on the couch praying. I began to feel as though the Holy Spirit was trying to tell me something. As I got quiet to listen He said, "Revelation 12:11." I felt it more than heard it. And I repeated it, "Revelation 12:11." I walked over to Michele and said, "Look up Revelation 12:11." She opened one of the numerous Bibles we always had close at hand and looked it up.

"Read it to me." I said.

"They overcame him (the great dragon, the ancient serpent, called the devil or Satan who leads the whole world astray. Rev. 11:9) by the blood of the Lamb and the Word of their testimony, and they did not love their lives so much as to shrink from death." I listened intently and as Michele read the words the Holy Spirit nudged me again. I stood still in the middle of our living room as the verse she read echoed in my head. Slowly, as if by divine interpretation, the meaning of the verse began to come to me.

"The blood of the Lamb AND the word of their testimony!" I said out loud. "That's it!" In an instant I knew it without a shadow of a doubt. Our enemy was indeed real and he was trying to destroy us. Not by making us sick. Not by keeping us awake, and not by scaring our daughter. No, what he wanted was the only thing that could ultimately destroy us. He wanted us to quit believing God was who He said He was. Satan wanted us to deny the truth about Jesus. Our life with God had begun when we first believed that Jesus Christ was our Savior! We had since learned that He was born to a virgin, lived a sinless life and was crucified, died, was buried, and was resurrected from the dead! And now He is alive and well and overseeing the fulfillment of God's plan for all mankind. It was like a news flash on TV!

"We interrupt this program to bring you this very important late breaking news item! It has just been learned by those close to the source that the devil, satan, is trying his best to steal from you the most precious gift you have ever and will ever possess! Yes, it's true, make no mistake about it; the devil wants you to turn your back on Jesus and renounce God's plan of salvation through Christ!"

The devil wanted us to admit that God's forgiveness and salvation, which is available only through Jesus, was just one more empty spiritual philosophy filled with wonderful and grandiose but empty promises. It was then that I got angry. For the first time in a year I knew who my enemy was and what he was up to. The Holy Spirit reminded me that I am not to fear the one who kills the body but only the One who can destroy the body and send the soul to hell.

I stood in the middle of the living room and issued a challenge. I don't recommend this remedy to anyone but it is what I said. "I know who you are and I know what you want. But I want you to know that no matter what you do to me, my wife or my baby, I will go to my grave proclaiming Jesus Christ is Lord, to the glory of God the Father! So go ahead, do your thing, but I'll never renounce Jesus Christ. He is my Lord and my Savior, now and forever!" I remember it as if it happened last night. I stood in the living room and worshiped God. I thanked Him for His love, His forgiveness, and His revelation. I thanked Him for Jesus, for sending Him to die on the cross for my sins so I could be reconciled to God. Knowing I was His child through my faith in Jesus Christ I knew I would spend the limitless eons of eternity immersed in the peaceful power of God's holy presence. Michele and I then prayed for Lindsey and put her back to bed. She slept through the night.

Nearly a week later we were sitting down to supper and I noticed Michele was not coughing. She remarked that we had been eating without any complications. We agreed that Lindsey had been sleeping through the night. We realized then that we were free! It had been one of the most miserable years of our life. And yet it was also the most profoundly exciting year. We had met God. He was real. He loved us. And we were His children through our faith in the life, death, and resurrection of His son, Jesus Christ!

Chapter 3

Closing the Door

I am the door. If anyone enters by me, he will be saved, and will go in and out and find pasture (John 10:9).

We were born again. The phrase was difficult to define but the experience was not. We were different. We thought differently, we felt differently, and we acted differently. At first we didn't understand the concept completely. It sounded too religious. But Michele and I never considered ourselves to be religious.

The main difference was that we felt closer to God. He was there. Life was good. Life was good, there was peace, and we had new purpose. We saw that self-indulgence was no longer life's highest goal. We no longer sought peace and fulfillment in pleasing ourselves. We knew to live successfully we must live as God wanted us to live. We were determined to trust Him to guide us as we prayed daily to know His will and to be empowered by His Spirit to accomplish it.

As we prayed for guidance our lifestyle began to change rapidly. Some of the changes were not our choice. Our business, which had been doing quite well, began to slip away. Sales dropped steadily two years in a row. We were forced to change locations twice. Our gross sales dropped way off and without explanation. The market had not changed, we had not tried anything new or different. It was as though our business was just melting away.

Our personal income reflected that slide dramatically. During that period we cut back on employees, increased advertising, and pumped twelve thousand dollars of our savings into the business to keep it going, all for nothing. As income dropped expenses seemed to increase. Inventory had to be bought so we would still have something to sell, the rent still had to be paid, utilities continued as before, etc. The picture was not pretty. We were fearful of the trend and spent many sleepless nights praying to know God's will. We sought the counsel of several successful Christian businessmen. Their advice was godly and good. But it did not change our situation.

Finally, after more than two years of pumping the bilge to stay afloat, we started talking about the inevitable. Closing the door. After praying about it we decided I should take a weekend off and fast and pray to find God's perfect will in the situation. A friend who had a condo was going to be out of town for a week. It looked like a good opportunity so I asked if I could borrow his condo while he was gone so I could get alone with God. I locked myself in on Friday night.

I spent the time praying and reading the Bible, and pacing. I could not find a comfortable chair in the place. I couldn't sleep either night. And I had no interest in eating. And to make matters even more frustrating I wasn't getting any revelation from God. I had on many occasions felt strong

Closing the Door

impressions and even had times of feeling divinely guided to certain places at certain times to speak with specific people. This time however, I heard and felt nothing spiritual at all. Until Sunday afternoon.

As I was speaking aloud with God, whining again actually, I grew increasingly more frustrated. Finally, I blurted out, "God please tell me, what should we do?" And I heard a voice say,

"Close the door, lock it up, and walk away."

"What?" I asked out loud.

"Close the door, lock it up, and walk away." The voice was clear.

I repeated His words in the form of a question, "Close the door lock it up and walk away?"

And there was silence. I stared at the front door of the condo. I just sat there and stared at it. Like a man struggling to solve a riddle. I stared at the doorknob and the solid door and in my mind saw it open and close several times. It was a very easy, graceful, movement. It opened and it closed. It wasn't difficult, it was easy, it happened all day long. Doors opened and closed every day all the time all over the world. As they did this people were able to pass, both into and out of. It shouldn't be a big deal. I shook myself from the vision and methodically began to collect my things and pack my bag.

Driving home an hour later I argued with God. I said things like, "But how does one do that, just close the door and walk away?" And things like, "What are people going to think?" And, "You mean just close it up? Does that mean bankruptcy?" I felt I had heard from God but I certainly did not know how one just closed the door of his seven-year-old business, and walked away.

When I arrived home I told Michele what I had heard from God. She wasn't very impressed. I couldn't really blame her. It was new territory for us. This new land was completely uncharted, and a little frightening.

The next day I called a friend of mine who was an attorney and asked him what he knew about bankruptcy. He said that wasn't his forte and recommended I call a hotshot bankruptcy firm he knew of in another city. So I did.

The next day on the phone I explained to the bankruptcy attorney the situation and asked for advice. He asked me several questions regarding my business. Things like assets and liabilities, earnings and accounts payable, IRS and sales tax. The kind of questions that can make the owner of a dying business very nervous. And they succeeded in doing just that. When I asked about bankruptcy he said, "No, I wouldn't bother with it if I was you."

"What do you mean?" I asked.

"Well, that might not be a very good tack for you to take, given the specifics of your situation," he replied.

"Oh? Well, then what do you suggest?" I managed to ask weakly.

"Well, if I was you I would probably just close the door, lock it up, and walk away."

I was frozen for a moment. Had I heard him correctly? Had he just spoken the words I thought I heard God say in my friend's condo two days ago? I asked the attorney to repeat his advice.

"Well, it would not benefit you to file bankruptcy, and it would just cost you more money, which you don't have." Then he repeated the phrase again. "I'd just close the door, lock it up, and walk away."

I began to laugh self-consciously and thanked him for his input. God was guiding us in truly miraculous ways. I wasn't sure how closing the business was going to be accomplished. But we were soon to learn through many similar events, God is faithful to disclose His will to those who are willing to pursue Him until they know it.

Chapter 4

Suffering in Perspective

These things I have spoken to you, that in me you may have peace. In the world you will have tribulation; but be of good cheer, I have overcome the world (John 16:33).

I sat on the couch praying. Actually I wasn't praying, I was complaining. I was whining to God about how terrible my life was since I had become a Christian. I know it sounds ridiculous, but it seemed to be true. Before I was a Christian I had the world on a string. I was going places. Business was booming, and the future was indeed bright.

But as Michele and I often say, "After we met Jesus all hell broke loose." Our business began to fail. Our health declined rapidly. Our baby daughter began to have nightmares and seizures as she slept. Our friends abandoned us, and all of our family members' thought we were weird. It was bizarre.

I sat on the couch moaning and groaning, "So, this is the abundant life, huh Lord? Big whoop-dee-do!" I was miserable. And it was all God's fault.

My observation was a judgment error many Christians make. I thought when a person finally got right with God, life was supposed to be pain free. Not so. Life is life. Even though God forgave my rebellion, I still lived in a world filled with rebellious people. Sometimes they made my life more difficult than it needed to be. I had learned to accept the apostle Paul's view of suffering. He said, "Momentary light affliction is creating in us a weight of eternal glory far beyond all comparison." On that particular day though, I was fed up with all the trials. So, I sat there whining to God about how bad life had become since I had become a member of His household.

I paused for a moment in my lament and sat staring at the floor. I held my hands clasped together, fingers interlocked, in the posture of prayer. And the Holy Spirit spoke to me.

"Look at your hands." He said it gently but firmly. I knew it would be best to do what He said. So, I looked at my hands. First the backs of them and then I turned them up so I could see the palms. Noticing nothing significant, I thought, "Okay, where's this going?"

He spoke again. "Look at them real good."

Again, I did as I was told. But I saw nothing.

"Do you see any scars on those hands?" His voice was gentle but it carried in its tone the uncomfortable weight of conviction. Immediately I understood and felt ashamed.

"Don't complain to me about your suffering," He said. "Remember, I know what suffering is. Just be thankful that I haven't asked you to suffer for me like I suffered for you."

"Yes, Lord." I replied quietly.

Suffering in Perspective

His words took me back in time. I saw the cross again for a moment. It was hideous and grotesque. Those nails had splintered skin as well as wood. He was stuck up there like a dying animal after the hunt. His face was bruised and swollen from the soldiers' fists and blood ran in red streams from the puncture wounds on His head. It mingled with his sweat and stung His eyes. But He could not wipe it away. Bearing down on the stiff metal rods driven so mercilessly by the hammer's cruel blows, the weight of his body threatened to rip His shoulders from their sockets. The pain was unbearable as He pushed up on the spike in His feet so He could gasp for one more lung full of air. I could not hold back my tears as I remembered how my Lord and my God died. He did it for me.

I thought too of the momentary light affliction that Paul suffered, and was reminded that it included being beaten, and jailed more than once, and that on one occasion he had been stoned by an angry mob and left for dead! I was embarrassed that I had considered myself as persecuted as Paul. As I began to thank Jesus for His grace, His provision, and His protection, I had to admit; I really didn't know a thing about suffering.

Chapter 5

God Rents the Truck

But seek first the Kingdom of God and His righteousness and all these things will be added to you (Matthew 6:33).

Our walk with God has been filled with divinely orchestrated events of truly miraculous proportions. As we continued to do what we believed God had shown us to do, we continued to see His work in our affairs. Scripture speaks of the similarity of the working of the Holy Spirit and the blowing of the wind. We do not see the wind, but we do see the results of the wind's work. Leaves rustle, kites fly, and sailboats move silently across the bay. But we do not see the force that accomplishes these things. In the same way, the Holy Spirit works in our lives, and even though we don't see Him, we see the results of His work.

When we closed our retail business I went to work for a friend. I was like a fish out of water working for him and even though I did poorly, he graciously promised to keep me on his payroll until I knew exactly what God wanted me to do next. Michele and I continued to minister to the people attending our weekly Bible study and we prayed for His will to be revealed.

Closing the business without claiming bankruptcy meant we brought all the unpaid bills with us. Even though my new job paid well and I was making a very good salary, we never had enough money to go around. We had always been faithful to creditors and were proud of the fact that in more than thirteen years of marriage we had never bounced a check. But as we were trying to pay bills from the business as well as household bills on one income, every month we fell further behind. We knew things had to change but we didn't know how or what to change. So we prayed.

Six months after closing the business we had accumulated more than twenty-five thousand dollars of unsecured debt and my salary was not keeping up. We kept praying hard to know God's will.

We discussed our situation over pizza with a friend one night. He offered a refreshing evaluation of the subject.

"There's no doubt you're called to ministry, so it seems to me that you have three choices. Number one, you can quit your job and hang a sign on the door and call yourself a church. You have been meeting on Saturday nights for more than two years. And these twenty-five or thirty people look to you as their pastor. So, you are a church, you just don't want to admit it." That choice was overwhelming to Michele and to me. Neither of us was equipped to take on the responsibility for the people.

"Number two, you can go to work for a church, doing whatever they need done, submit yourself to the pastor, and learn your trade through on the job training." Not a bad suggestion, but not very good either because I didn't know any pastor who was willing to train me.

"And, number three, you can go to college, and prepare for a career in church work." As he offered the last suggestion, I felt an exciting little jab deep within me. Could I really go to college? At my age? I had recently celebrated my thirty-ninth birthday! I was married, had a small child, was in debt up to my ear lobes, and had been a D/F student in high school more than twenty years earlier. But even as I said "No" to suggestion number three, in my heart of hearts, I was excited about the remote possibility of attending college.

"Well, what do you think?" my friend asked. After more discussion, we agreed to pray about it for a week and then meet again.

As the week went by I talked to God about the situation. I felt like I was rediscovering a desire that I had buried a long time ago. I had always wanted to go to college. But I never felt good enough or smart enough to make it. Since I began my life with God I often thought about what it might be like to study God's word in a college setting. The Holy Spirit reminded me that when I was discharged from the Army sixteen years before I had thought about going to college, but I had been too afraid and had received no encouragement to do so at the time. As I prayed during the week the smoldering coal of desire was fanned into a small flame.

We met again, munching pizza as we talked. "Well, what do you think?" our friend asked. "What did God say?"

"I want to go to college." I replied. Then I told everyone what I had been going through during the week and how I felt it was a real possibility that God might be saying, "Go to school." I quickly added, "But I'm not sure. Financially it's impossible and it sounds sort of selfish to me."

Again my friend responded wisely. "Why don't you pray this week and ask God to either fulfill your desire to go to college or to take the desire away from you and replace it with His desire for you?" Again we agreed to pray and meet one more time.

This time I asked God to tell Michele if it was His will for me to go to college. I did not want to drag her off to some undisclosed place for an undetermined length of time, while I pursued some hair-brained idea that I thought God had told me to pursue. I had a long history of being a little impulsive. In our marriage, Michele was the more methodical and practical one. I wanted her to hear from God and to know what His will was for us.

When we met the following week we were asked to share what we felt God had spoken to us during our prayer time. I graciously allowed Michele to share her feelings first. She looked at our friends and then at me and said, "I know it sounds crazy, but I think this idea is from God."

Very quickly I asked, "What do you mean, from God?"

"Well I think you're supposed to go to college. I don't know how we will pull it off. But I think it's God's plan and if it is, well, He will make it happen. Right?"

By the time she finished speaking my head was spinning with delight. I was so happy I could hardly speak.

Things can happen fast when God's will is unfolding in your life. The next two months was a flurry of activity. First we contacted the college and were accepted. Then we visited

God Rents the Truck

the campus and met with the registrar. We looked at student housing and were approved for moving in. We packed the house, put a lot of stuff in storage, and planned to leave on our daughter's fifth birthday. Even though we didn't have any money, we were excited. We were in debt up to our nostrils and the college didn't have a financial assistance package. But we were excited. Our excitement as only partly due to the idea of going to college. But more importantly we felt like we heard from God on another major issue and were now pursuing His will for our lives, our marriage, and our ministry.

Before we left home all the details of the move started to fall into place. First someone offered to pay my tuition for the first year. Wow! We had a big yard sale two weekends in a row, sold a lot of stuff, and made a substantial amount of money. And we figured I could use my last paycheck to pay for the truck rental and the gas to drive the four hundred miles to our new home.

The morning before we were scheduled to drive out I paid a visit to my former boss to collect my last check. It was actually my first check, which he had held back when I went to work for him almost a year before.

He was surprised to see me walk into the shop that morning. I told him we were ready to load the truck and that I had come to pick up my last check.

"What do you mean?" he looked concerned as he spoke.

"You know, your policy to hold back the first check on a new employee."

"Oh, no, don't you remember," he stated, "You were so broke when you came to work for me that I paid you that first week."

His words hit me like a blast of winter wind and I shuddered. And I remembered, oh, how I wish I hadn't remembered! But I did. He had paid me that first week. It was a long time ago but I remembered it distinctly. I stood there, my mind reeling, trying to quiet my labored breathing and wondering what to do next.

"What are you going to do?" my friend asked.

"I don't know," I managed to say, feeling like I was about to faint.

He asked again, "What are going to do?"

"I'm going to go get my truck. My whole house is packed in boxes and I'm supposed to be on campus in two days." I couldn't believe it. How was I going to accomplish this? The credit cards were maxed out. I had a little cash but not enough to pay for the truck and pay the rent when we arrived on campus.

"I'm going to go get my truck." I said again. He looked at me pathetically as I turned and walked slowly out of the shop.

As I stood before the truck rental counter waiting for the man to finish the paper work, the question kept racing through my mind, "What are you going to do?" I kept repeating like a trained parrot, "I'm going to get my truck."

God Rents the Truck

Then the phone rang. The rental guy picked it up and, as incredible as it may seem, I heard him speak the following words.

"Yes, uh, yes sir, he's here. Yep gettin' a twenty-four footer. Well, if you want to. Yes sir that'll be fine. Okay, thank you. Have a nice day." He turned around and walked over to the counter smiling. Locking eyes with me he said matter-of-factly, "Well, your truck's paid for."

"What?" I stammered.

"Your truck's paid for," he repeated. And I watched in shock as he completed the rest of the paper work. He filled in every blank on the page, including the full amount collected for the rental.

He handed me the keys and, still smiling, said, "Have a safe trip."

I climbed into the cab with tears seeping out of the corners of my eyes. I couldn't speak. The joy that was in my heart was beyond my ability to comprehend or describe.

God is awesome! Michele and I often say, "God will blow your mind, if you give Him the chance! He knows your need before you can ask.

Chapter 6

Formulas or Faith?

Come to Me, all you who labor and are heavy laden and I will give you rest (Matthew 11:28).

Michele and I are not religious. As we understand the term, it refers to behavior that is ritualistic and which is carried out routinely. We studied and participated in a wide variety of spiritual religions before we were introduced to Jesus Christ. Many doctrines required rituals and repetitive acts of devotion and service. The completion of those rituals guaranteed the devotee a share of the rewards. As we look back on our involvement in them we see that they embodied the essence of the religious. They all preached a self-aggrandizing doctrine; "If you do (you fill in the blank) you will move the unseen impersonal forces of nature and those forces will produce—for you."

As children we attended Sunday church services with our families. We did so ritualistically. Christianity was something we did on Sunday, like watching NFL football. It wasn't something we pursued during the week. It certainly wasn't something we thought much about. We just did it because we were told that's what you did on Sunday morning. Although the purpose of ritual church attendance was never explained to me when I was a child I assume the idea was, if we were faithful enough in our Sunday morning ritual, God would smile on us and life would be peaceful and happy. As I think about it now, it was religion pure and simple.

However, our encounter with Jesus Christ was something more than a religious thing. When we surrendered our lives to his Lordship we became partakers of divine truth. We didn't work for it, we didn't earn it, God simply bestowed it upon us. We knew deep in our hearts that Jesus Christ died for our sin in order to reconcile us to the sinless God, the creator and sustainer of the universe. This truth wasn't something we studied diligently before hand so we could apply it and receive benefits. It came in the form of revelation, after we, through a Holy Spirit inspired act of faith, confessed our sin and asked Christ Jesus to be our savior and Lord.

Being born again, through surrender by faith to the grace of God made us partakers of divine truth. That experience had nothing to do with a Sunday church service. It was instead a personal encounter with the personification of divine truth. We had met Jesus Christ through divine revelation. We had embraced what appeared to be a religious concept yet upon doing so we entered into a personal relationship with a living God. This was not religion, this was relationship.

God is a relational being. He is three distinct persons functioning inseparably in perfect unity. Christians know this idea to be the trinity. Even though the term is not recorded in the Bible, the concept is scripturally valid and accepted among Bible believing Christians of many different doctrinal persuasions.

Formulas or Faith?

God is relational and every living thing He created was intended to function in relational harmony with every other thing. Man's relationship with God was designed to be harmonious also. Man's part in that harmony is knowing God's will and doing it. If mankind as a race could do that successfully the world would be a wonderful place in which to live.

Too often Christians make the same mistake their earlier spiritual counterparts, the Old Testament nation of Israel, made. They erroneously believe obeying rules, adhering to doctrine, and performing rituals, will either, A. prove their worthiness, B. earn God's approval, or C. pacify God's wrath. However, God is not impressed with any of these things. He doesn't want impersonal ritualism from His children. He wants a loving relationship with them.

God knows ritualism is the result of religion, whereas relationship is the result of loving appreciation. He said if we loved Him we would obey Him. And He said His commandments were not burdensome. How could love be a burden? Love will sacrifice. But ritualistic sacrifice is not necessarily inspired by love. In the Old Testament God spoke through the prophets saying He hated Israel's sacrifices. This was because they were trying to manipulate God. They knew they had been bad and were trying to pay Him off. It proved they were blind to His love for them. He wanted them to love Him because He wanted to bestow His love on them. But the people of Israel wanted to be like their secular neighbors. They loved everything but God. Then when convicted of their rebellion by the priests or prophets they attempted to placate God through the sacrificial system. It was the age-old mistake of exchanging relationship for religion. The modern parallel consists of exchanging faithfulness for formulas.

Life with God

Michele and I found that our growing love for God created in us a desire to serve Him. We wanted to please Him because we loved Him, not out of fear of His retaliation if we didn't. The lover always desires to honor, and to serve his beloved.

Within a couple years of our conversion experience an odd belief system began to creep into our relationship. We started to get religious. Before college we had been taught by Bible teachers from many different backgrounds. And most of them preached an "If-Then" doctrine. It goes like this. If you want God to do (___) for you then you must first do (___) for God. At the time we did not recognize the error. We simply fell into it. We started to think we could manipulate God's grace. That is, if we performed a little faith ritual, then God would do what we wanted or needed Him to do.

Such thinking implies God doesn't know what to do, or that He cannot or won't do it if I don't do something first to wake Him up from His sovereign slumber. All of which says He cannot be trusted! It is ridiculous of course to question any aspect of God's flawless character.

Michele and I were in the midst of adopting and applying such injurious doctrine when I sat down to write a tithe check one Sunday morning. I had been unable to find work after moving to another city to go to college. I looked at my checkbook nervously as I sat at my desk praying. The balance was a meager sixty dollars. Four hundred dollars worth of monthly bills was due in the coming week. The question nagging me was, "Would God really supply?

Being a tither since my conversion, I said, "Well Lord it'll have to be an offering this week 'cause I already tithed on this balance last week and I haven't earned anything this week. So, what'll it be?" I sat still and listened. As I waited, thinking the

Formulas or Faith?

suitable offering could be in the five to ten dollar range I felt a very strong impression to make the check for twenty dollars! Out loud I said, "But, Lord, this is the offering, above the tithe! And twenty dollars is thirty percent! The tithe is only ten percent!" Imagine the impertinence of lecturing God on His tithe principle!

I was clearly exasperated by the thought of giving up twenty dollars. As I sat agonizing over the amount a strange and wonderful thing happened. I heard God speak in an audible voice! Please don't think I'm a heretic. If it hasn't happened to you, it does sound weird. But weirder things have happened. I know it really happened so I make no apology for it. He spoke audibly and said, "Do not base your relationship with me on formulas, but on faithfulness," there was a very brief pause, then He added, "MY Faithfulness." Not mine but God's faithfulness to me! Let me ask you a question dear reader. Whose faithfulness would you like to lean on in a time of uncertainty, yours, mine, or God's?

As He spoke, the room where I was sitting was filled with the most peaceful presence I have ever felt. It was like being in the middle of a cloud, far away from all the concerns of life on earth. The air was as clear as a winter day in the mountains. The sensation of breathing it in is still indescribable in human language! Peace permeated every square inch of the room. I didn't want to move for fear of disturbing it! I sat still and let the peace of His presence comfort me. It was simply glorious. Several minutes passed as I sat silently savoring the waves of soul soothing peace washing over me.

When I regained my senses, I wrote a check for twenty dollars without the slightest thought of the balance in the checkbook or the amount of bills that were due. I had neither the slightest intention of testing God nor concern for getting any money back. I wrote it because I knew God loved me and was faithful to me. He was only asking me to trust Him. This He desired I do that I might discover how truly trustworthy He is. When His children learn how much He loves them there will be no more trials in life. Trials will be transformed into opportunities to witness His incomparable grace, His enduring mercy, and His endless provision.

By the following Friday more than four hundred dollars had been given to Michele and I through several different sources! We had not asked one person for a dime. The bills were paid because God was faithful!

Formulas are not bad. They can produce results! But, if we use the Bible as a book of magic formulas to conjure up solutions to our needs, we have made a terrible mistake. Rituals are reserved for religious men who are desperate to move the impersonal forces of nature for personal gain. However, God, whom we address as Heavenly Father, wants His children to interact with Him and to learn to trust Him. His desire is to have a relationship with His children. It is out of that relationship that His blessings naturally flow into the lives of his children.

Chapter 7

God Still Heals

He laid hands on every one of them and healed them (Luke 4:40).

We started a Bible study in our home within weeks after our deliverance. We opened our home to anyone who wanted to listen to me expound on the Word of God. We met on Saturday night. People came from miles around. We had twenty-five to thirty people every week. They came at seven and stayed until two or three a.m.! They surrendered to Jesus, got filled with the Holy Spirit, and were physically healed! It was glorious. At the same time I became involved with the Full Gospel Businessmen's Fellowship. In addition to being vice president of our local chapter I traveled around the state sharing my testimony and praying for anyone for any reason. God did some awesome things during those meetings. Physical healing, emotional healing, restoration of relationships, and a flow of the gifts of the Holy Spirit were evident.

The following two incidents illustrate that wonderful period. Both of them took place in our home. In one, the sick one was our two-year-old daughter. Michele phoned me at work one morning to express her concern of the fever Lindsey had. We agreed in prayer for her healing while we were on the phone. I suggested she call me back if Lindsey's condition did not improve. After offering a few words of encouragement to Michele I hung up. I continued to pray throughout the morning as my schedule allowed. Just after lunch the phone rang again. It was Michele again sadly reporting that the fever had worsened. Her concern had grown into fear. We prayed again and I told her I would come home early if necessary.

I left work early that day, praying as I drove home. I reminded God that He was the healer and that He said we could pray believing, call for the elders of the church, or lay hands on the sick and they would recover. Those are God-given options for dealing with sickness according to the Word of God. I believe it.

When I walked into the house I was not pleased with the scene that greeted me. Michele was sitting on the couch cradling Lindsey in her arms. My beautiful happy little Lindsey was lifeless. Her arms were dangling pathetically and her head remained motionless as I approached her. Her pretty blond hair was stuck to her face by the perspiration that covered her. I was struck with fear when I saw her condition. And then before I was overwhelmed by the fear, anger rose up in me. My anger was not with my wife, whom I trust completely to do the right thing at the right time, or with God, for neglecting to protect my daughter. No, I knew who my enemy was and I remembered what the Holy Spirit had told me about his tactics. The Bible says we should not be ignorant of Satan's devices.

I sat down next to Michele and touched my baby's face to wipe her hair away from her eyes. Her skin was hot to touch! Not warm, hot! It was too hot to touch! She was completely still; her eyes were nearly closed, as if trying to keep them open caused her pain. Again, for a moment fear gripped me. But I fought to ignore it and to concentrate on the fever. I looked at Michele and said, "Let's pray."

I laid my hands on Lindsey's little arms and rebuked the fever. I told it to go, to leave her body, and never come back. Together, my wife and I commanded life, health, and normal functioning to come back to her body. We told the body temperature to normalize. As we did this an incredible thing occurred. Her skin began to cool! Even as we were praying, her skin began to cool. We could feel it in our hands. We looked at each other in shocked amazement!

Lindsey's skin continued to cool rapidly. We laid her on the bed and sat with her. As we quietly praised God, offering thanks, she improved by the minute. Within fifteens minutes her skin was cool and she was sitting up on the bed smiling as she does when waking up from a nap. Thirty minutes after praying for her she was literally jumping up and down on the bed giggling!

I do not know why this healing amazes me. But it does. Even today more than twenty years later, having seen many people healed dramatically through the prayers of God's people, I am still amazed when God heals someone. But the truth is God still heals!

Another significant healing incident is worth noting because of the peculiar way it happened. It took place during one of our Saturday night home meetings. As was our habit, after sharing insights from the Bible we would break into groups, one for men and one for women, and address prayer requests. On this particular night a young woman asked Michele and I to pray for her. She wanted a private meeting so we took her into Lindsay's bedroom. Lindsey was asleep in her bed.

The woman told us she had suffered from low back pain since she was five years old. She had been asleep on the back seat of her parents' car when they were hit by another car. At the hospital she was treated for minor cuts and bruises and released. Since her accident she had suffered from back pain and had taken various medications for relief. She was in her late twenties the night we prayed for her and said she always had pain in her back.

Michele explained to her that we were going to pray for her and that Michele would lay her hands on the woman's lower back as we prayed. She agreed that would be okay. So, I said, "Okay then, let's pray." As I started to pray Michele moved to touch the woman's back, but before either was accomplished we heard her back crack. It was not a whisper; it was very noticeable to all three of us! The woman responded with a startled, "Oh, my!" Michele and I looked at each other puzzled. Did God really heal her before we could either pray or lay hands on her? You betcha!

The woman was smiling from ear to ear and saying things like, "Wow, I'm healed!" and "The pain, it's gone!" She was bending and twisting trying to find the pain but it was gone! Her closing comment was the best of all. "For the first time in my life I do not have any pain in my back!"

We witnessed many of these kinds of healings. Like the time Michele prayed for a young woman who was shopping in our retail store with her sister. God healed her and she was a member of a religious group that didn't even believe in divine healing! These encounters convinced us God still heals!

The most dramatic demonstration of God's power I have witnessed, through my hands, occurred in a prison. I had been invited by a friend to share my testimony with the inmates. I took my guitar and sang songs and told the story of my quest for God. It was a wonderful night. As I shared my story I felt the power of God's presence touching me deeply. I had sensations of power and peace coursing through my body as I spoke. At times I felt like I wasn't really doing the speaking but that someone else was speaking through me.

The time came to invite the inmates to come forward for prayer. Many of them responded. I began praying with a small group who had come up on the stage. While I prayed the rest of the ministry team traveling with me met with different ones in small groups scattered around the prison chapel. After about thirty minutes one of my ministry team members approached me on the stage and whispered in my ear, "There's a man down there who wants you to pray for him." I responded politely, "Okay, I'll be down there in a minute."

Ten minutes later the team member approached me again, "Hey, this guy is waiting for you to pray for him." This time my team member was a little more firm. I turned to see the man he was speaking of. He stood in front of his wheelchair. His neck was wrapped in a padded cervical collar and he was staring at the floor leaning on his cane. He looked to be in his late sixties or early seventies. "Oh boy," I groaned. "Uh, Lord," I said weakly. "I don't have the faith for that man's healing, this one will have to be all you." It wasn't until much later that I recognized the arrogance of that statement. The Holy Spirit gently replied, "Good, now that you're out of the way, watch me heal him." I walked hesitantly over to the man awaiting me.

His friend, who had wheeled him into the chapel greeted me and said, "He's not doing so good. He's had two strokes and a heart attack in the last couple of months." I didn't say it but if you could have read my mind you would have heard me groan, "Oh, great."

I bent down to intercept his eyes as he stared at the floor. There was a little trickle of drool dripping from one corner of his mouth. The whites of his eyes were yellow from either disease or age, I wasn't sure which. Trying to be as cheerful as I could be under the circumstances, I announced bravely, "Brother, what you need is a Jesus overhaul." He responded with a grunt.

I placed both of my hands on the top of his head as I began to pray, asking God to restore his health. I systematically moved down his body praying for each major organ or muscle group as I went. The experience was like a dream. I felt involved and yet disengaged at the same time. It was as if someone was praying through me. I knew later it was the Holy Spirit.

As I regained my composure I noticed I was kneeling on the floor in front of him with my hands on a pair of blue hospital slippers that covered his feet. Tears were running down my cheeks and though I hadn't been aware of it, I had been crying. Finishing my prayer I self-consciously wiped away the tears and stood up. The old man standing before me didn't look changed at all. I looked into his eyes again and said gently, "Now, brother, sometimes you have to receive your healing by acting in faith, so I want you to try to take a few steps for me, if you can, okay?" As I spoke, to my amazement, he lifted up his head, straightened his back and started to stride confidently across the front of the chapel! He didn't shuffle his feet like I expected him to do. No, he just took off, walking across that auditorium like a twenty-year-old! I was visibly shaken and started to follow after him hoping that I might catch him if he fell. But he wasn't about to fall. He was standing as erect and walking as lively as anyone in the room. The crowd exploded in applause and praise!

When he got to the end of the auditorium he turned around and started walking back toward me. I was standing in front of his wheelchair and sensing he was coming back to sit in it, I put my hand up like I was stopping traffic and said, "Don't you go near that wheelchair." He looked at me and threw his cane into the seat of the wheel chair. "Oh, don't worry about me," he smirked; I'm not going near that thing again. I don't need it! Jesus healed me!" The crowd was applauding and praising God as the once disabled man walked out of the room under his own power. His friend walked out behind him shaking his head in unbelief.

As I rode home that night with one of my best friends I could feel a powerful presence in the car with us. It was the same combination of excitement and peace I first felt more than twenty years before one night on the beach. I have felt it many times since. I assume it is the manifest presence of the Holy Spirit. My friend, feeling it too, turned to me as we rode and said, "That wasn't you up there on the stage tonight. That was..." he paused for a moment trying to find the right words and then finished, "that was incredible." It's true, as incredible as it seems, God still heals!

Many times since then I have had opportunities to pray for healing. And many times I have seen God do truly miraculous things! What frustrates me though is as often as I have seen them healed I have also seen them not healed. Many times I have asked God, "Why?" And to this day I don't really know the answer. I'd like to say its because God does not want to heal everyone I pray for. But that doesn't seem consistent with what His word says about healing. In the Old Testament He speaks of Himself as the God who sent His word and healed all our diseases. In the New Testament, Jesus tells us believers will lay hands on the sick and they will recover. For several years I was frustrated by the inconsistent results of my prayers to the point where I wanted to quit praying for sick people. But I knew this was not right either. Again, we're told in the Bible if anyone is sick we should call for the elders of the church and they can anoint the sick one with oil, pray for his healing, and he will be healed.

However, I now have come to believe the problem is one of responsibility. There is a big difference between my responsibility in the healing process and God's responsibility. I am not wise enough to critique God's responsibility so I will limit my thoughts to mine. As I read the Bible I see God has given me, as a believer, certain responsibilities. One of those responsibilities is to pray for the sick. However, I do not think He wants me to take on the responsibility for the outcome of my praying, that's up to Him. The procedure is simple. I do the praying, He does the healing. The story of Meshach, Shadrach, and Abednego is a good illustration of this.

The story is found in the book of Daniel chapter three. It seems King Nebuchadnezzar wanted the boys to worship him and not worship anyone but him. They did not agree so he threatened to throw them into a blazing furnace to prove he was the King and had the last word on the matter. He even challenged them by saying, "Now which god do you think will rescue you from my punishment?" In verse sixteen the boys answered and said something like, "We do not need to defend ourselves in this matter. If we are thrown into the fire, the God we serve is able to save us from it and He will rescue us from your hand. But even if He does not, we want you to know we will not serve your gods or worship them or you." Now right there the boys were stating in a round about way, "no matter what God does or doesn't do, we're going to do what He told us to do." In other words they were not going to obey God and do as He commanded them if and only if

He responded the way they thought He should. They were prepared to do what He said, no matter what the eventual outcome was to be. And in this case the outcome might have been death by being burned alive! The story ends on a praiseworthy note, however, because even though they were relegated to the furnace, God did protect them. The soldiers who threw them into the fire were burned to death, but the boys didn't even smell like smoke when they came out of the furnace!

My point in telling this story is this. I no longer try to figure out what God may or may not do as I pray for someone to be physically healed. All I am required to do is to pray, and to believe it is God's will to heal the person I'm praying for. I cannot take responsibility for their healing. One more illustration from my life makes the point clear.

When a friend of mine was disabled in an accident I told him I would pray for him until he was healed. I had been praying for several years but he was still not healed. Many people prayed for him for many years. But he was not healed. So, I began to be less diligent in my intercession for him. One day as I was enjoying my quiet time in the word and prayer the Holy Spirit said to me, "You aren't praying for your friend anymore. Why is that?" I replied matter-of-factly, "Well after so many years of praying without results, I thought maybe it was not your will for him to be healed."

Quietly the Holy Spirit asked, "What are you going to say to him when he calls you to tell you he is healed and to thank you for praying for him all these years?" I did not know how to respond. So, I just sat there and thought about it, for a long time.

You see, the Holy Spirit was trying to help me see the difference between my responsibility and His. I am responsible to pray and to believe it is God's will to heal the sick. Just as I am to cast out demons, speak with tongues, turn the other cheek and go the extra mile. As a disciple of Jesus Christ and one who walks with God, I am to do what I am told to do and let God take the credit for the results.

Does God still heal people miraculously? Without a doubt. That's why I continue to pray for the sick. I pray expecting God to do a miracle. And sometimes He does!

Chapter 8

God and the Tax Man

For your Father knows the things you have need of before you ask (Matthew 6:8).

Is there any institution that strikes more terror in the heart of the American workingman or woman than the IRS? Well, perhaps there is, but for me one year, that was it! Fear is one emotion that will put the spotlight on one's need for God pretty quickly. You may doubt the existence of God or your need for Him when life is going well. But when push goes to shove and you're up against the ropes being pummeled by our opponent, the existence of God can become very important to you. As this situation taught me; nothing takes God by surprise. He does not have moments when all of a sudden He encounters something that overwhelms Him. He never wrings His hands and says, "Oh, gosh, now what am I going to do?" Even though God had a plan in this case, too, I was just beginning to learn that He could be relied upon even in the most intimidating circumstances.

The year we closed our business our accountant reassured us that everything would be okay and that he would handle everything including closing out the books and taking care of the legal requirements. For the remainder of that year I worked for a friend while trying to hear from God what I was to do next. By the time April of the following year rolled around my accountant informed me by phone that he was going to file for an extension because he had not finished all that he needed to do on our account. "No problem," I said. I was sure he knew what he was doing.

In August we moved to another city to attend college, and I had forgotten all about the extension. Actually I had forgotten not only the extension, I had also forgotten the accountant, and any hope of getting out from under the mountain of debt we were in. When, in September, I remembered that we had not filed our income tax for the previous year a cold stabbing fear pierced my heart. "Oh, no, the IRS!" I winced.

I called the accountant's office and was informed he was no longer with the firm! "Oh, great!" I replied. I explained my situation to the man on the phone, and he said he would get back to me. Two weeks went by and I heard nothing. So, I called again. This time the man said my account had been turned over to another person and that person had been fired for his poor performance.

"Yuck." I said. This was not going well. But I was reassured by the man on the phone he would take care of it and get back to me. He didn't.

So, by early October I had not filed with the IRS, was in debt up to my eyebrows, and was earning a whopping ninety dollars a week working part time. Add to this Michele reminding me I needed to do something about the IRS and one can see why I was beginning to twitch.

I went to a Dynamics of Spiritual Life class one day and the professor reminded us that, "God will not leave you hanging." He went on to say, "He is faithful and will handle it even when no else can." I sat there listening and the reality of his statements settled on me like a warm blanket on a chilly winter night.

I went home after class and announced to Michele that God knew the situation and that He had it all under control. I probably added something inspiring like, "And if we cannot trust God, whom can we trust?"

One Sunday afternoon in late November I received a phone call from the accountant's office. The man apologized profusely as he explained that my file had apparently been lost during the shuffle of employees. He was the new branch manager and had come in on Sunday to look over the office and ended up cleaning out a file cabinet. In the bottom of the cabinet behind the bottom drawer he found my file which, he said, "by the looks of it has been laying down there for several months."

He added, "And, by the way, I went ahead and re-figured your income tax and instead of owing a couple thousand you will get a refund of over three hundred dollars!" Three hundred dollars was like three thousand in my destitute condition! I was overjoyed. He said I could hold off paying him until I had my refund check in my hand! More good news.

Since we had already learned the value of not using credit cards, even in a crunch, Christmas was a bit lean in our home that year. We received the refund check on December twenty-sixth!

God can be trusted! The wonderful thing to remember about our God is that He is a personal God. He is not an absentee owner who wound up the world like a clock and walked away to do something more important in some distant corner of the galaxy! He is involved in our lives. He is called "Heavenly Father." Heavenly, means other than earthly, and Father, means the one who takes care of us, provides for us, and protects us. He is involved in our lives, whether we know it or not. It is to our advantage to know it, acknowledge it, and work in harmony with Him to bring about our highest good.

The following year we had another divine intervention concerning the tax man. This time I found out I owed the IRS just under four hundred dollars! I have never owed the IRS money at the end of a year. This was a new one for me. Four hundred dollars was like a million to a full time college student making ninety dollars a week who was in debt up to his mustache and had a wife and child to feed!

But, I was learning that God was faithful. I was the guy who had been told by God's audible voice to base my relationship with Him on His Faithfulness, not on formulas. So, I made a deal with Him. I said, "Okay, Lord, I don't have any money. You know it as well as I do. So, here's the deal; you can supply the money or I will write the IRS an IOU unless you tell me to do something differently. I'll pray and seek your will on this until April fifteenth. If you don't tell me to do anything different and I don't have any more money than I have now, I'll send them a check for twenty-five dollars, and an I.O.U.

I prayed that prayer every week from January through March. I did not hear anything different from God so I was prepared to go ahead with my plan. When April fifteenth rolled around we had a friend staying with us for the night.

God and the Tax Man

He was in full time ministry and was on his way to a conference in a city west of us. We had not seen him since we left home more than a year earlier. After supper and much warm conversation, we all prepared for bed. Michele and I went to our bedroom. I told her I was going to drive to the post office to mail the check to the IRS because I wanted it to be postmarked that night. I stepped out the back door and walked across the wet lawn to the car.

I sat in the driveway and prayed. "Lord I'm going to write this check for twenty-five dollars unless you tell me differently." I had already written the IOU on a piece of notebook paper. As I sat listening for His voice, I heard him say, "Make the check out for fifty dollars."

"Fifty dollars! Aw, Lord, c'mon, fifty dollars?" I whined.

"Make the check out for fifty dollars." He said again.

"Okay, here goes." I said, once again hoping He knew what He was doing.

I wrote the check for fifty dollars and scratched through the twenty-five on the IOU and wrote in above it, "fifty dollars." Then I started the car and drove to the post office.

When I returned home I went in through the back door to the bedroom. As I came in Michele asked, "Did you see that loaf of bread Mick's daughter baked us?"

"Yes," I answered.

"Well when I removed it from the bag there was an envelope in it," she said sleepily.

"Oh, yeah, what's in it?" I asked.

Life with God

"I don't know, I didn't open it. I put it up there on the dresser," she explained.

I went to the dresser and opened the envelope. In it was a card expressing her prayers for success in college. But the card was not the only thing in the envelope. It also contained a check, the amount of which was hard to read because of the tears in my eyes. The amount of the check was fifty dollars!

The old song says, "He's got the whole world in His hands." Do you believe it? The longer I walk with Him the more amazed I am by the practicality of His loving provision. We received a reply from the IRS about a month later, thanking me for my note and explaining to me they had re-figured my tax return and found a mistake. Instead of owing them nearly four hundred dollars, we only owed them two hundred. I had already paid them fifty, so our balance was one hundred fifty dollars. Which I paid off by August of that same year.

I know scripture says we are to avoid laziness and to work hard, but I wonder how often we miss seeing God's miraculous provision because we strive so hard to provide for ourselves.

Chapter 9

Honey and Powdered Milk

If you then, being evil, know how to give good gifts to your children, how much more will your Father who is in heaven give good things to those who ask Him! (Matthew 6:11)

God will provide. We were certainly learning that first hand. Sometimes His method of provision was a little out of the ordinary, but we were finding out He always provided. We sat at the table one day staring at our lunch. Popcorn and water. It wasn't by choice that we had settled on the meal. It was all we had! That was the week our five-year-old Lindsey had opened the door on an almost empty refrigerator. Standing there looking into the barren metal shelves she remarked bluntly, "Daddy, if we don't get some food pretty soon, we're going to die." Of course things weren't that bad. But the refrigerator was empty. Our grocery budget during that time was twenty-five dollars per week.

At lunch after my morning theology class, I called the girls to the table for a family meeting.

"We have to agree on something." I began, "We need to decide why we are in this sad condition. Now, the way I see it, either God brought us here to college or He didn't. And we need to decide and agree one way or the other. He either did or He didn't. And if He did then He knows our condition, how much money I make and how much money we need. And if He did call us to college then He didn't do that to trick us or to make us look like fools. Right?" I looked at them both.

"Right." Michele said convincingly.

"Right, daddy," five-year-old Lindsey added smiling knowingly.

I continued, "And if He did bring us here then He is going to provide for us, right?"

"Right."

"Right."

"Then if we know He brought us here and we know He is going to provide, our response should be praise and thanksgiving, right?"

Again they agreed in unison.

"Okay then, from now on we're going to thank Him everyday for all that he has given us and all we know He is going to give us." We then bowed our heads and gave our heart-felt thanks for the popcorn and the water. We did that same thing everyday. It didn't matter what was or wasn't on the dinner table. Every day we praised God and thanked Him for providing for us everything we needed including all the

Honey and Powdered Milk

money to pay all our bills on time with plenty of money left over to help others and to do fun things.

One truly wonderful incident from this time in our life involved our one vice. Coffee with half-and-half. It was the only treat Michele and I allowed ourselves. We spent about three dollars a month on coffee and two dollars a month on half and half. Neither of us were heavy coffee drinkers, we just enjoyed a cup in the morning, and especially during the winter months. Then a friend of ours, with British heritage, taught us to enjoy hot tea, with honey and half and half. We enjoyed it until we ran out of honey and could no longer afford the half and half.

Michele was trying to be cheerful about this latest shortage and continued to thank God for His provision. But she really did miss her honey and half-and-half. Tea wasn't quite the same without it. She was thankful we had powdered milk. But then we eventually ran out of that too. One day during her personal devotions, she groaned, "God, it sure would be nice to have some honey and milk."

The following Saturday I happened to be out in the yard when a car pulled into a friend's driveway across the street. The lady went to the door and began to knock on it. I knew they were not at home. I called over to her and explained that they had left for a vacation. She thanked me and got back in her car, but instead of driving off she pulled into our driveway. She rolled down her window and asked, "Do you know someone that could use some food?"

"Uh, yes, I do." I said.

"Well if you'll get that box off the floor behind the seat, it's yours."

Life with God

"Sure," I said as I stepped quickly to the back door of her car.

"Thanks." she said. And then she backed out of the driveway and drove away.

I carried the box into the house and called Michele.

"Come here and look what the Lord gave us."

The box contained two two-pound boxes of powdered milk and two five-pound jars of honey, in addition to some other food. My wife stood there in unbelief shaking her head. God is so good. I wonder how much He might do for us if we would let Him? Michele says this incident means more to her than some of the bigger things God has done for us. It seems a small request to make of the God who created the universe. But that is what makes this incident so special. It proves God is interested in the minor details of our life. And how cool is that?

Chapter 10

God, the Auto Mechanic

*The works that I do in My Father's name,
they bear witness of Me (John 10:25).*

It may sound odd to think of God as an automobile mechanic. And rightly so. First of all most people do not enjoy thinking about auto mechanics. A visit with your favorite guy means there's trouble and it's going to cost you to have the trouble fixed. And secondly, most of us don't want to think of the Holy God wiping greasy hands on an orange shop rag. It sounds a bit sacrilegious. Its true though, people who fix broken cars are auto mechanics. And the following incident would clearly indicate that God knows how to fix cars. Although, I'm sure He doesn't soil His hands in the process!

We affectionately called the car "Rusty." It was a small sporty model that had certainly seen better days. But the old saying reminds us, "don't look a gift horse in the mouth." For a long time I wasn't sure what "they" meant when they said that. However, I eventually learned that in the days of buying and selling horses, the buyer was always encouraged to look at the horse's teeth to determine not only his age but also his current health. If one was in desperate need of a horse and was offered a horse as a free gift, the recipient was encouraged to simply be happy with the gift. It was considered insulting to the benefactor to inspect the horse's teeth to see if it was a good horse!

When our friend told us God had told him to give us the car, we were pleased as punch to get it. We didn't even look at the rust crumbling away from the wheel wells and the bottoms of the doors. That meant the rainwater that came in through the rust holes in the top of the doors would drain quicker! The engine seemed to run okay, and the tires were good. The faded and peeling light blue paint didn't bother us. The brakes were adequate. So what if the air conditioner didn't work and we lived in Florida. During the ten months of summer we just rolled all the windows down and let the humidity-laden hot air whistle through the car. It didn't cool us but we were thankful for having the car. And so what if the heater fogged up the front windshield in the winter? It only meant we had to drive with one of the windows down so the fog would clear, which of course defeated the purpose of the heater. Who cared? The Florida winters weren't too severe anyway.

Rusty had been a good reliable car the first year. Other than the minor maintenance that one expected with an older high mileage American car, we were able to keep the car on the road with minimum expense. That is, until we went to college and saw our already strained financial resources melt like a pop-sickle in the hot Florida sun.

One cold rainy winter morning as I was preparing to go to a class, Rusty refused to wake up from his slumbers. I tried time and again to coax life into his motor but even when it started it wouldn't idle. If I gave it lots of pedal it would rev up, but as soon as I took my foot off the accelerator,

Rusty would cough and sputter and wheeze and resume his slumber.

I didn't feel like walking to class in the rain so I prayed and begged God to let me get to class dry. I started Rusty again and revved the motor to keep it running. I'm not sure the neighbors appreciated the early morning serenade and I promised God that I would apologize to them later in the day. Rusty and I then limped over to the parking lot of the building where my morning class was to meet. When I pulled into a parking place, I didn't need to turn the key to the off position. Rusty merely closed his eyes and went back to sleep. I took a moment to thank God that I didn't have to walk in the winter rain, and went to class.

Over the next two weeks I did all that one with no money could do to figure out the malady Rusty was suffering from. I talked to friends who were mechanical. I wasn't and am not to this day. Like most smart people, I avoid working in areas for which I have no aptitude. And I have never understood the secret mysteries of infernal combustion engines. On the rare occasion when I have attempted to work on one I usually managed to make matters worse. So, I call my friends who possess whatever spiritual gift it takes to enjoy covering your hands with grease and cutting your knuckles sharp metal objects! I received numerous diagnoses for Rusty's illness. And most included the mention of money, and the rebuilding of carburetors and the like. However, at the time I was not in a position to pay for anything that was not essential to life support, like food. So, we prayed.

The prayer went something like this. "Well, Lord, you know our need. Rusty's illness doesn't take you by surprise. And you know we don't have the money to give to the mechanic that thinks he knows what the problem is but may not really know until he gets in there and takes it apart. So, here's the deal, Lord. At your discretion, you can either send someone to correctly diagnose the problem and fix it for free, give us some money so we can take it to the mechanic, have it fixed, and pay him for the parts and labor, or fix it yourself." It was really that simple. And I added, "And let us know what you're going to do so we can follow up on the plan."

For the next two weeks I walked to class, passing by Rusty sitting there in his spot in the parking lot. He didn't look so pathetic when he was surrounded by all the other cars. But in the early morning when I went for my run, there he was all alone, rust ravaged and forlorn, keeping his silent vigil.

From time to time, the other students would ask me, "Did you get your car fixed yet?" When I would answer, "No," they would look at me sympathetically and say something encouraging like, "Well, keep praying."

Then one Saturday, two weeks after I had parked Rusty, Lindsey and I went for a walk. Michele was at work in the campus bookstore. As we approached Rusty in the parking lot, looking rustier than ever, I felt a strong impulse to try to start the car. The idea was so strong, I didn't question it. It was as if the thought did not originate with me. It was more like I was being told to get in the car and start it.

Lindsey and I got in the car. It was cold and musty inside because the windows had been rolled up for two weeks. I took my keys out of my pocket and inserted the right one into the side of the steering column. I turned it, the engine started to turn over, and I pumped the gas pedal. "Vrum!" Rusty roared, clearing his throat. I pumped the gas pedal revving the motor, "Vrum, vrum, vrum," Rusty responded. I was shocked! Delighted, but shocked. So, I took my foot off the pedal to see if he would idle for me. And he did, the tachometer needle was pointing right at 1000 rpm!

Lindsey and I sat there is silent awe and listened to Rusty hum. After a few moments I pulled the console mounted shifter backward into Drive and slowly pushed down on the accelerator. We began moving across the deserted parking lot. We smiled at each other sharing the delightful moment. We drove Rusty around the parking lot slowly at first. Then we deliberately passed the big picture window of the campus bookstore, waving to Michele as we did. We went around again and the second time we passed the bookstore she came out to smile incredulously and wave. I didn't stop to chat for fear we would not get Rusty going again. Finally on the third pass we exited the parking lot and joined the traffic on the highway. Rusty continued to hum happily. I took him all the way to sixty miles an hour. He didn't cough or protest once. He simply obeyed as if it was his pleasure to do so!

To my knowledge, no one came to the parking lot to fix Rusty. If they had they certainly would have told us when they had finished. No one else had a key so even if their intentions were good they couldn't do a thing. No, we have a simple answer to any that ask us why we think God would bother himself with our broken car. The answer is, God loves us. He is big enough and good enough to fix broken cars, to heal damaged bodies, and to restore strained marriages. The real question that must be asked is; "Are you willing to give the problem to God and to joyously and confidently expect Him to do something about it?"

We drove Rusty for another year and had no more problems. We did not spend one more dime on repairs! We renamed him Rusty the God-mobile. And, to make a good story even better, we eventually sold Rusty to another student who literally begged us to let him buy the car!

Is God good, or what?

It may sound odd to think God fixes cars. But over and over He has proven He is faithful to supply all of our needs. In doing so His compassionate concern for His children is verified.

Chapter 11

The Tale of Two Fifties

Give and it will be given to you: good measure, pressed down, shaken together, and running over will be put into your bosom. For with the same measure you use, it will be measured back to you (Luke 6:38).

The man or woman who walks with God walks against the main stream of popular convention. To defy convention can stretch an individual's faith in God to the snapping point. But to do so on a daily basis will make his confidence in God strong. The biblical references to this sometimes painful and almost always frightening process are numerous. In some cases the individual succeeds in maintaining his integrity. In other cases, he fails miserably. For instance, in Eve's encounter with the serpent in the Garden of Eden, she failed to remain true to God's expectations of her. Adam then followed suit, and the rest is, as we say, history.

By contrast, Jesus remained faithful in His garden challenge at Gethsemane, and God's will was accomplished. Jesus was very familiar with the process of walking against the flow of the crowd, though. It was only minutes after his baptism by

John the Baptist in the Jordan River that he passed His first faith test! Scripture records that he was immediately led by the Spirit into the wilderness to be tempted by the devil! But he fasted for forty days first. Then while he was at his weakest (or strongest, depending on your view of fasting) satan came to him to tempt him. Yet Jesus successfully overcame every one of satan's attempts to get him to turn his back on God's will.

Standing strong in faith when it is most difficult has its rewards. Not the least of which is the strengthening of one's faith. In fact it is when Christians face their biggest challenges that they get to see God act in truly miraculous ways. For in truth though faith is nurtured in the solitude of study and prayer, it is often strengthened in conflict, and most clearly proven in total hopelessness. We cannot experience the magnificence of God's will unless we surrender to it completely and without reservation.

When God directed Michele and I to college, from a practical point, there was simply no way we could go. We were in our late thirties, we had a five-year-old daughter, and we were so deeply in debt that we couldn't pay the rent on time. As we sought the counsel of our friends, many said we were crazy. Some implied I was acting irresponsibly selfish. Several asked, "How can you afford it?" We simply answered, "We can't, but we really feel this is what God wants us to do."

We prayed hard and long to determine if we were hearing God's voice about college. We did not enter into it quickly or without some anxiety. It was a monumental challenge. But let us share with you what God did. It doesn't make sense even now as we recount it. But we lived it and know its true.

The first hurdle in our lane was tuition. When we were praying about the move to another city to go to college God had told me not to ask anyone for money. He said He wanted us to see how well he could provide for us. It sounded crazy. But it also sounded like God to us. We had no reserve capital and the college we were directed to had no financial aid program because it was not yet accredited. All the students attending were making other arrangements to pay their bill. Just before we left I calculated that we needed approximately two hundred dollars extra each month for the first year just to pay my tuition! Two hundred dollars was a huge amount of money for us in our condition. But God had a plan.

One week before we were to leave home my pastor invited me to breakfast. As I nervously pushed my eggs around with my fork, I talked excitedly about school and studying God's word. Suddenly my pastor asked, "So, have you prepared a budget yet?"

"Yes, I have." I answered confidently.

"Have you calculated what tuition is going to cost?" he continued.

"Well, yes I have. In addition to our living expenses tuition will be about two hundred a month."

He smiled broadly. "Well, my wife and I have been praying and that's the figure we believe God is directing us to support you with each month for the first year."

I thought I was going to faint. I stared at him knowing I was supposed to say, "thank you," but my lip was trembling so I knew I would cry if I opened my mouth. Tears filled my eyes and spilled out onto my cheeks. He looked as uncomfortable as I felt. Finally I managed to say it. "Thank you."

So, even though I had no money and no job in the new city, and although I did not know a soul there, and even though the college had no financial aid program and was not yet eligible for state grants, God had already supplied my tuition for the first year!

I mentioned in another chapter of this book how God paid for our rental truck the day I went to pick it up and discovered I had no money. However, the next six years were filled with stories like these two.

One of the most mind-boggling money miracles of all is the tale of our friend. We called him/her our friend because we did not know his/her real name. Still don't. But for the first forty months we were in college this anonymous person sent us two money orders every month. One came on the first of the month and the other came on the fifteenth. For forty months! Each money order was for eighty dollars. One hundred sixty dollars a month for forty months is six thousand four hundred dollars! Whoever it was wanted to remain anonymous so we have never tried to uncover their identity. Jesus says when we give quietly and anonymously our Father will see it and reward us. If we give to be seen and appreciated by men, the Jesus says that is our reward.

One other incident worth noting involved the "joyful giving and receiving" cycle. It went like this. We had moved again. This time it was on to graduate school where all our bills doubled including tuition. Having no more contacts in this, our second, new city than we had in the first new city, I put out a total of seventeen resumes. I had ten years management experience, had owned my own businesses, was an exemplary employee and had a wonderful track record. But I couldn't get a job! One manager told me that he wouldn't hire me because I had more experience than he did, and he didn't want to lose his job!

The Tale of Two Fifties

One Saturday afternoon as we were preparing to have dinner with some people who lived on campus, a friend walked into my living room and handed me two fifty dollar bills. Bear in mind, during those lean years my family of three was spending about twenty-five dollars a week on groceries!

The man handing me the two fifty dollar bills was a student like myself. But I had only one child, he had three! And he did not have a job either. I looked at him in unbelief.

"John!" I stammered, "What are you doing?"

"I'm being obedient to the Lord," he replied weakly.

"But you have three kids, I only have one." I argued.

"It doesn't matter. I'm just doing what I'm supposed to do, okay?" He sounded convinced.

I took the two bills from him, a little embarrassed. "Okay, if you're sure?" I locked eyes with him.

"I'm sure."

"Wow," I thought to myself, "now we have money for some groceries. Wait 'til I tell Michele." She was elated, to say the least.

The next morning was Sunday. We were going to visit another new church. We had only been in town for a couple months and were still visiting churches in the area trying to find a new church home. I took one of the fifty's with me so we could stop by the grocery store on the way home.

Life with God

The worship in the church was real good. We enjoyed ourselves. When the time came to collect the offering the pastor was very straightforward and low key. I would like to ask you to pray and ask God what you should give today." Then he bowed his head and prayed for us to hear from God what we should put in the basket as it was passed around.

As I began to pray the Holy Spirit said, "Put it in there."

I tried to pretend I didn't hear him.

"Put it in there." He said again.

"Lord!" I whined quietly in protest.

"Who gave you that money?" He asked me firmly.

"You did." I answered quickly.

"That's right," he said softly, "and I have much more."

So I rolled up the fifty-dollar bill discreetly and when the offering basket came to me I slipped it in real quick. I didn't want either Michele or Lindsey to see me do it.

After church we got in the car and drove back toward our home on campus. As we neared the intersection where the grocery store stood, instead of turning into the parking lot, I drove right on by.

"Where are you going?" Michele asked.

"Home." I answered politely.

"Why?" she retorted.

"To get some money."

"I thought you brought one of those fifty's with you?"

"I did."

"Well then, why are you going home?" her question hung in dead air for a moment, while I struggled not to say what I knew I must say. When I didn't reply to her last question, she moaned, "Oh no! Hon, you didn't?"

"Yep." I sighed.

"You put it in the offering?"

"Yep."

"Are you sure it was the Lord?" And though she asked the question, she knew the answer. It wasn't the first time he had directed one of us to give money to someone we didn't know.

"Well, I sure wouldn't give fifty dollars away, if it wasn't." I replied.

"I know, I know," she said confidently.

So we went home, grabbed the other fifty-dollar bill, and headed back to the grocery store.

It's funny, really. People who don't walk against the grain don't understand it. We had been given one hundred dollars on Saturday, by someone just as broke as we were, and who claimed to be obeying God. Then we were asked by the God who gave it to us to give half of it away on Sunday, which we did.

His purpose was to help us strengthen our faith. He wanted us to learn a valuable lesson. That is, God can and will supply our needs if we let Him. Oh, by the way, the next day we received a check in the mail for two hundred dollars!

Chapter 12

God Pays the Rent

*According to your faith let it be to you
(Matthew 9:29).*

Quite often people ask us for details regarding living with no apparent income. It is truly amazing. We hardly kept track during the initial stages of this wonderful life with God. It was all so new to us. And it was all so frightening. We had grown up in the America of the past. The America where one worked to earn his living. Government handouts were for someone else. The protestant work ethic said, "If you want to eat, work." We even started a ministry to those in need, which we called Faith Works Ministries. We didn't mind helping but we expected you to do something, however small to earn your way in the world. We believed given the opportunity most people wanted to work, in the interest of self-respect.

Yet there were times during the early days of our life with God when we could not find work. Michele and I have always worked. Since childhood, it was just something we did. But there were times when we sent out literally dozens of resumes, followed up on many interviews, even to the point of bothering potential employers. The only explanation we can give is that God wanted to show us how well He could provide for us. And truly we would not trade the experience for a month off with pay! Through our experience we have learned first hand that God is not only able but also willing to meet every need we have.

One of the happiest stories we tell involves some good friends we had first met while in under grad school. Like us they had been married for more than ten years, were established in their relationship with each other and were committed to following hard after God's plan for their lives. After under grad school He had directed them back to the denomination they had been asked to leave when they received the baptism of the Holy Spirit several years earlier. Just before we moved to Virginia Beach to attend Regent University, they moved on to Lutheran seminary.

The event happened like this. Michele and I had been praying about going home for Easter break. As usual finances were tight. I was earning about one hundred dollars a week working in the Media Center at Regent U. We knew we had a sizable tax return refund coming. We were prepared to pay off a large bill we owed to another friend who had bought a car for us. We owed them one thousand dollars. The original agreement was made six months earlier and knowing what our tax refund could be, we agreed to pay them when we got the return. We don't like owing people money. Considering all of this, we asked God to give us fifty dollars to confirm our request to travel home on Easter break.

When the tax refund came, I called the friend who was now pastoring a church in Texas. I told him that we had the money to pay them. He insisted the money had been a gift, not a loan. And he refused to take any money from us.

God Pays the Rent

Wow, we had asked for fifty dollars and God had supplied one thousand! We were ecstatic. But my darling wife quickly reminded me we had asked for fifty dollars not one thousand. I knew she was right. We therefore used the thousand to pay some other bills, and to have some much-needed maintenance done on the car. It's amazing how quickly one can spend one thousand dollars when he's broke!

We kept praying for the fifty dollars to come before we left for home. And true to form, at the last minute, a day before we were to leave for home Michele's mother sent us a check for fifty dollars. That was it. We prepared for our trip.

Now understand dear friend, we prayed this way because we had no extra money to pay for gas, the rent would be due when we got back, and we would lose income by taking the time off from work. We are very careful not to be foolish with our money or to be presumptuous of God's plan. We had learned that if we pray, seeking His will, not our own, He would direct us. We had also learned that His will for us is always better than our will for ourselves. If what we want is not what He wants for us then what we want is not the best.

Having received the money from Michele's mother we felt released to go home, enjoy our friends, and the Florida sunshine. In effect, we felt God was saying to us, "even though the rent is due, it is okay for you to spend money on your trip."

While home we were given money from some friends who had decided to support us monthly. They wanted to give us twenty-five dollars a month. And they wanted to pay the first six months in advance. Wow! One hundred fifty dollars. Thank you, Lord! In addition another person gave us one hundred dollars. All of which was further confirmation to us that it was God's will for us to go home.

But back to the rent and our friends at seminary. When we arrived home from our Easter break, six days later, I went to the mailbox to get the bills, and to look for more of God's miraculous gifts. We had decided to put the one hundred fifty dollars our friends had given us toward the rent. We needed only three hundred more to pay it. As I sorted through the mail, I came across a letter from our friends in seminary. I always enjoyed hearing from them. I consider John to be one of the most dedicated Christians I know. He is an inspiration to me for his personal discipline, piety, and humility. When I opened the letter a check fell out. I quickly glanced at the check, which was for thirty dollars and read the letter. He explained how they had wanted to bless us for some time and God had finally provided a way for them to do so. The note was brief. I picked up the check again and smiled, thinking warmly of our friendship over the years. Then my eyes were redirected to the amount. Could it be true? I thought my eyes were playing tricks on me, so I handed the check to Michele who was unpacking suitcases.

"How much is that check made out for?" I asked.

"Hon!" she said sounding shocked, "It's for three hundred dollars!"

I spun around in my chair and grabbed the check from her. It was true. The amount was not thirty dollars. It was three hundred dollars! I knew the struggle they had been going through to pay their bills. They had three kids. Seminary was expensive. How in the world could they afford to give us such a generous gift? I immediately wrote a thank you note, expressing both our elation and our thanks.

Once again, we had learned that God is truly able! Even though He had given us the confirmation through the fifty dollars from Michele's mother, we still wondered if going home for a break was wise use of His resources. But here was living proof. A check for the exact amount needed to pay the rent! I sometimes wonder what would have happened had we not gone home. Maybe He wanted us to go home so we could collect the other one hundred fifty. Isn't God incredible?

But the story is even more amazing when you hear John's side of it. When he and his family visited us several months later I told him how significant his check had been. He smiled and told us the following story.

Unknown to them, his wife was one of many beneficiaries in an elderly uncle's sizable insurance policy. The good man had died and a five-figure check had been sent to them in the mail. They were tithers and our name was very near the top of the list of people they wanted to bless. John sat down and began praying about the best way to disperse the tithe from the check. When he came to our name he decided to give us two hundred dollars. As he started to write out the check, he just did not feel at peace with the amount. So, he continued writing other checks to other people in need. Eventually he came back to our name and again he tried writing the check for two hundred dollars. He just couldn't do it. He said he didn't know why, but he felt sure the Lord was directing him to make the check for more. He went to bed that night praying about the correct amount. When he awoke in the morning, he was sure he was supposed to make the check for three hundred dollars. So, he did.

I was just about to burst with joy as I listened to him tell his story. When he was finished I spoke up.

"John, you wrote the check for three hundred dollars because two hundred would not have paid our rent! We were short exactly three hundred dollars!"

We laughed and sat for hours discussing God's loving attention to details. He truly does know our needs. Even before we can ask, He is ready to supply them. He wants us to learn to trust Him.

I will add that in all the years we have seen God provide we have never tried to pray for our will to be done in any situation. We always pray, "God let your will be done here, that you may be glorified." For me to pray any other way presumes I know God's will in a specific situation. I have found many times I do not know His will. In fact, I find I most clearly discern His will in retrospect, after seeing it manifest. Does this mean I do not have the miracle producing faith needed to properly direct my affairs and the affairs of those in my household? No, I believe it means something more. It means I am a child of God, I am not God. He knows best and as I take the time to seek His will in any situation He will guide me so I can pray in harmony with His will. It means I know He is faithful, and that my faith is weak and quite often it is self-indulgent. It means what I need more than anything else in the world is a very close personal and intimate relationship with the God who is all-powerful and who has my best interest at heart.

Chapter 13

Miraculous Tuition

*But the very hairs of your head are all numbered.
Do not fear therefore; you are of more value than
many sparrows (Luke 12:7).*

At times, our life with God has been frustrating. The reason for this frustration is found in one of the basic differences between God and man. God knows the future. Man does not. God knows what you, and I, are going to be doing three months and three years from now. He knows when each of us will marry and when each of us will die. As disciples of His it feels good to know He knows the future. Since we don't. But sometimes our fear of the unknown over rules our willingness to trust God with the details.

Perhaps the most difficult time of trusting God came about as we waited for Him to do something about my tuition to graduate school. By the time we arrived at Regent University we had come to know God was faithful. He had provided for us in truly miraculous ways many times. But the move from Florida to Virginia had taxed our already strained resources to the point of exhaustion.

The cost of housing, and tuition had more than doubled. I had put out numerous resumes in the Tidewater area. No one wanted me. I was told by one manager that I was more qualified than himself and the manager was afraid of losing his job to me. In frustration I had even answered an ad for help at a gas station. But I just could not go through with the interview. Pulling into the gas station I prayed, "Lord, I'm willing to work here, pumping gas and changing oil, but I find it hard to believe that you brought me all this way just so I could work in a gas station."

Finally, after a frightening three months of unemployment, as I was having photocopies made at the university Media Center, I was asked to apply for a job opening in the audiovisual department. So I did and went to work making $4.75 an hour and working 20 hours a week! That's ninety-five dollars a week! Which was not a lot of money in 1991. Not for a family of three. But there seemed to be nothing else to do.

Many surprises awaited me at Regent. One was finding out I could not have the scholarship I hoped to get because it was only available to returning students. It was very frustrating, to say the least. It meant I would have to take a summer course, pay for it as best I could and try to get the twenty-five percent discount as a returning student in the fall. The course cost about five hundred dollars. We had no money. Where would we get that kind of money?

But as I said God knew the future. He had a plan that would meet our need. He knew who was going to supply the funds for tuition, and when. I sure wish He would have told us. It would have made the next three months a lot easier. The main point though is that the money came, in time. In a casual conversation with a friend I mentioned our dilemma. The friend responded without hesitation, "Well, we can give it to you." I stammered and said, "Yes, well, you could, but that's a lot of money." The friend went on to say that he and his wife had prayed that they might be able to help us when we went to college. Here was the perfect opportunity. So, they sent the check, and I went to my first class.

The summer was hot enough but way too short for us Floridians. August was soon upon us and the time for registering for fall classes was just around the corner. But we had no more money than we had in January, when we arrived. There was still a chance for a twenty-five percent reduction in tuition but that left over twelve hundred dollars, plus the cost of books. It was due upon registration. Credit was not allowed, and if a class wasn't paid for by the third week of the quarter the class had to be dropped.

We prayed. Boy, did we pray. And I worried. During one of those worrisome days I was reminded of the time I had prayed in preparation for the move to Virginia. I stood praying for God to supernaturally provide for us in Virginia. As I did, the Holy Spirit interrupted me. "Don't pray for provision in Virginia Beach."

"What?" I replied.

"Don't pray for provision in Virginia Beach." He said again. AI have already provided for you in Virginia Beach. Pray instead that your faith will be strong enough that you will be able to enter into the provision I have already made for you there." I remember thinking then the word had an ominous ring to it. "Oh, no, here we go again." I envisioned more tests of faith. Tests make us strong, but they are usually no fun. In retrospect we often laugh at out trials. During them we could not even fake a grin.

Life with God

Just a couple days before class registration I was agonizing over the lack of funds. I kept searching the mailbox for clues or financial gifts. I even had a conversation with someone who suggested I apply for student loans. But I was determined that God was going to provide for us. After all, it was His idea that we go to college in the first place. I figured if He wanted it, He could certainly pay for it. I had heard a sermon once where the preacher said confidently, "God doesn't order what He cannot pay for." It sure sounded good to me! If He wanted me to attend graduate school then He could pay the bills. After all we had been through, with the closing our business four years earlier, I wasn't about to go into debt again.

The tension continued to build. The day before registration I was a nervous wreck. I went to check the mail. There was nothing. No money, no cards, nothing but the usual end of the month bills. What was I to do? In despair I walked out into the woods behind our apartment complex. It was a gray afternoon. The clouds were low and hung like a depressing wet blanket all round me. The rain was a fine mist. I didn't even feel it as I walked numbly through the pines. I just wandered, calling out to God. But He didn't answer. After an hour or so I slumped to the ground and began to weep. I was exhausted from months of praying for my faith to grow strong. But, I wasn't strong. I was weak. I felt alone, abandoned by God, in disparate need, and yet there was no relief in sight. "God," I moaned, "You called me here. You wanted me to come here; this was your idea. If you don't want me here then tell me. I'll leave now. I'll pack my family and go back home. I'll admit I missed it. I'll tell everyone. I'm not the big strong man of faith that others think I am." I let the self-pity flow; it mixed with my tears. Where was God? What was He doing? Didn't He see my condition?

Miraculous Tuition

I lay motionless on the ground until I had no more tears to cry. I got up and slowly walked home. I didn't know what to tell Michele. That was probably the hardest part. I had to tell my darling supportive wife, I had blown it. We had come on a wild goose chase. And it was time to go home. How that would happen I didn't know. We had no money.

The next morning I awakened at my usual time, five-thirty. I showered and dressed for work. It was registration day, but I would not be registering. The thought depressed me as I quietly made my coffee, filled my thermos, and slipped silently out of the house. As I rode the half-mile through the pines, I peddled my bike slowly. I was not in a hurry to get there today. I secretly wished I could just disappear. I wished that I could get suspended between home and work, and never show up at either place. But I arrived just like I had been doing five days a week for months.

I went through the routine of unlocking doors, turning on computers, making coffee, checking the night staff's work. I felt dull and emotionless. I did not look forward to seeing the bubbly faces of my young student staff. I didn't look forward to seeing people whose lives were going as they had planned.

Just before seven the phone rang, waking me from my discouragement. It was the Dean of the Library. She was the director of all Library Services, including the Media Center. She asked if I could come to her office right away. I said yes and left the Media Center. I walked into her office and immediately felt better. She was one of my favorite people on campus. Dignified, crisp, efficient, and friendly. She had the warm smile of your favorite elementary teacher, yet her eyes sparkled with the wisdom found only through many years of walking with God. She motioned for me to sit and asked if I would like a cup of coffee. I declined; my stomach was

Life with God

already in knots. She began slowly but spoke deliberately as if expecting I might miss what she was about to say.

"Mike, you know we have been trying to find a way of dividing the department. And we have appreciated your input into this matter. Well, I am happy to say the new plan has been finalized and approved. We have only one more area of concern."

"Yes, ma'am, that's nice." I tried to look interested.

"Well, we were wondering if you would like to have the new position? That is, the director's position."

"The director?" I managed to ask.

"Yes, that's right. We would like you to be the supervisor of the new audiovisual department. What do you think?"

"Uh, well, yes ma'am. That would be fine. I'm sure I could handle the job." I was trying my best to keep my thoughts off my registration day dilemma.

"We think you would do a wonderful job also. So, if you say yes I'll start the paperwork rolling."

"Yes. And thank you, ma'am, for considering me for the position." I was brightening a bit.

"Oh, and Mike," the dear and glorious lady continued, "That is a full time staff position, with salary and benefits."

"Yes, ma'am. Wonderful, thank you." I was getting excited.

"And," she continued, "One of the immediate benefits is a seventy-five percent tuition discount."

I nearly fainted! Had she said seventy-five percent? While I was collecting my thoughts, she continued,

"I have already spoken to the comptroller for you and you are all set to go sign up for classes. Just go upstairs right to the head of the line and get registered. She's expecting you."

Warm tears of joy and relief were sliding down my cheeks. I sat transfixed, smiling stupidly at my dear sweet angel who had just rescued me from the jaws of shame and embarrassment. I was free! My tuition was paid! One hundred percent, seventy-five percent from the staff discount and twenty-five percent from my academic scholarship. Praise be to God! He is faithful, even when I am not. Which is most of the time. My tuition was paid from that moment until the last class two years later!

God had a plan. He had directed us to Regent University with every intention of paying our tuition. He not only paid the tuition but he made certain that every other bill was paid as well. In all of our lean years we have never paid the rent late. God has allowed us to go to the very edge of the edge several times, but He has always come through for us. He can be trusted.

I stood on shaking legs, with tears staining my face, preparing to leave. The Dean extended her hand. "God bless you, Mike." She smiled as warmly as ever.
"Oh, thank you, ma'am, He has and He does." I could hardly contain my amazement. I floated out of her office. "What a grand and glorious God we serve!" I thought as I ascended the stairs to the registrar's office.

God not only knows our need but He plans to meet those needs. The hard part is that we do not know the future so we don't always see how He is going to meet those needs. So, we must learn to trust Him. Speaking through the prophet, in Jeremiah 29:11, God said, "For I know the thoughts that I think toward you, says the Lord, thoughts of peace and not of evil, to give you a future and a hope."

Chapter 14

Confusing the Priorities

By this My Father is glorified, that you bear much fruit; so you will be My disciples (John 15:8).

If there is one thing I struggle with, year after year, in my relationship with Jesus Christ, it is my habit of confusing the priorities. One would think after being a part of the wonderfully miraculous experiences Michele and I have encountered in our life with God, I would have learned by now to order my priorities correctly. Having been born again at the age of thirty-six, I'm beginning to think there is truth in the expression, "you can't teach an old dog new tricks." If I was a psalmist I might write (Mike's plea for understanding when learning, for the eighty-seventh time, his way is painful):

How long, O Lord, how long, before I learn from my mistakes?
Why, oh why, do I continue to make the same mistakes year after year?
Hear, oh stubborn heart, the Lord's way is best!" (Psalm 151)

Life with God

Pretty pathetic, huh? The truth is this; When my priorities are in order I am in the best of all possible positions to receive the best God has to offer. I read a poem once that stated it like this;

Enough that God my Father knows,
Nothing this faith can dim.
He gives the very best to those,
Who leave the choice with Him.

In speaking of priorities, Jesus, of course, is my role model. Scripture teaches us that "He learned obedience" through His suffering. In another place it says, "for the joy He knew was to come, He endured the cross, despising its shame." I can only vaguely imagine His struggle in the Garden at Gethsemane. His will was to do His father's will. But that night in the Garden, obedience meant enduring the brutal agony and public humiliation of death on a Roman cross! Jesus knew God's way is always best, even when it calls for personal pain. In my case, the suffering I endure is minimal and usually is a result of losing touch with God's priorities.

During one particular season of suffering I fell to the carpet of my office in my home crying out for relief. I was seeking deliverance from the frustration of financial lack, and the uncertainty of my professional future. Michele and Lindsey had gone to bed hours earlier, so the house was quiet, except for my groaning.

"Oh Lord," I moaned, "Help me understand. I am confused. I have worked hard, followed your guidance, been faithful to tithe and give above the tithe. I have worked for free when called to. I teach Sunday school, sing special music, have a midweek men's prayer meeting in my home, encourage others, rejoice with those who rejoice and weep with those who have suffered loss. What else can I do?"

Confusing the Priorities

All this whining, of course, is not for God's benefit; I could never inform Him of something that has escaped His omnipresent sight. But complaining can bring therapeutic relief to one's frustrations. And since David poured out his complaint in Psalm 142, I figured I had scriptural support for doing the same thing!

During my supplication I mentioned to God all the things I lacked and all the things I thought I needed to live the abundant life. These were things that would demonstrate to the world in which I lived that God was a good God who blesses His children abundantly. On the list were things like counseling clients who could pay for my services, especially those who could pay the full fee. A house for my darling wife to call her own was on the list. And a car that spent more time on the highway than it did in the repair shop. Braces for my teenage daughter's teeth and reading glasses for my wife, who kept saying, "I don't need glasses," while asking me to read a product label or recipe for her. But most of all, I needed clear direction for my life if what I was doing was not His will.

My time laid out on the floor passed slowly that night. But, the Holy Spirit finally spoke.

"Get a pencil and paper." He said. I got up and grabbed one of the numerous legal pads I always have lying around. I then sat down on the couch and waited for further instructions. I didn't have to wait long.

"Make a list of all the things you need." He said. I had no trouble with that exercise. I just wrote down all the items I had been crying about. I counted fifteen of them when I finished my list. He spoke again.

"Now put them in order of importance." I did as He directed. It took only five minutes. I was proud of my list and felt confident that we were really getting somewhere now. My elation was short lived, evaporating as He spoke again.

"Now, where am I on the list?" The silence that followed rang like a gong, shattering the stillness of the night.

"Oh, of course... uh, You, Lord ... You are right up here at the top of the list," I tried disparately to make it sound obvious while scribbling J-E-S-U-S in bold print at the top of the paper.

"Yep". That's where you are, Lord, right up there. I thought you meant, you know, material needs." Then I underlined, J-E-S-U-S, just so there would not be any misunderstanding between us.

"Good," He said, "you have done well. Now erase all the other items on the list."

"What? But Lord? Erase them?" I stammered. Knowing I had no choice, I put my eraser to the paper. Before I could finish the task, peace began to come. When I had finished erasing the list, all that was left was J-E-S-U-S.

"Now your priorities are correct and most beneficial for you." He said reassuringly. The softness of His voice removed all my anxiety just as easily as my eraser had removed the items on my list. "I have a wonderful plan for your life. And as you surrender your plans to me I will fulfill my plan for you. I know your needs before you do. I even know needs you have not thought of yet. And I will fulfill your needs. Trust me. You see, my plan for your life is always better than your plan."

Peace flooded the room. I knew He was with me. And I knew He knew everything about me. He knew my sinful past, my precarious present situation, and my wonderful future. He knew my plans as well as His plans for me. I remembered David's words from Psalm 23, "Even though I walk through the valley of the shadow of death, I will fear no evil, because you are with me." It is interesting that in the line previous to that statement, David had remarked that God "leads me on the paths of righteousness, for His name's sake." I began to see that following God will bring Him glory and yet at the same time it may take me through the valley of the shadow of death. Like David then, I must try to remember God is with me, even when things don't seem to be going my way.

And even now when I lose touch with His plans for me or when I find myself groaning my way through another frustrating situation, I remember the words the Holy Spirit spoke to me that night in my office, "My plans for you are always better than your plans for yourself."

God can be trusted. He is faithful. He has a plan for your life. It is a plan that will bring Him glory. For a human being there is no nobler endeavor than to surrender all thoughts of personal gain that he may be used by God to bring Him glory.

Chapter 15

More Than Enough

It is encouraging to realize the God we have to do business with is a very powerful God. He does things in a very big way. Look up into the sky on a cloudless night and you will quickly see what I mean! There are billions of stars up there. When you compare our home, Earth, to the rest of the known universe, it is a rather small planet in a very small solar system in a corner of the Milky Way Galaxy. Now remember, there are billions of stars in our galaxy and our galaxy is just one of billions of galaxies in the known universe! God is a big God!

One might not like to think too much about God being this big. After all, if He is this big, how small are we? I remember my first revelation of the bigness of God. It happened as I was praying and worshiping God. It is my habit to exalt God's majesty when I pray. To exalt means to build up or speak of something or someone in a big way. That is what I like to do when praying. As I was doing that one night in prayer, I began to get a picture of the hugeness of God. I began to see Him as if He was a mountain. As the scene began to develop I realized I was viewing the mountain from a distance. From my vantage point, many miles away, the mountain appeared to be no taller than the space between my thumb and forefinger, which I held up in front of my eye to make my measurement.

As I began to move toward the mountain, it began to get bigger. The closer I got to it, the larger it became. Closer and closer I came and larger and larger it became. Pretty soon the mountain had grown to its full size. As I stood at the base of it and looked up, I could not see much of the mountain at all. God was that big compared to me!

I felt so small as to be insignificant. I felt like a grain of sand on the beach. My life was meaningless. I was nothing. No one had heard of me before I was born. And no one would remember me fifty years after I was dead. The concept was sobering, to say the least. Then, my feelings of worthlessness began to give way to feelings of vulnerability. Vulnerability moved on to feelings of intimidation and impending doom. Within moments, I experienced the fear associated with being truly insignificant in the presence of the One who wielded unlimited power and ruled with unchallenged authority.

As I considered my unacceptable condition in the presence of One as glorious as this, I had but one thought, mercy. Just before I cried out for mercy from this threatening tyrant, an odd thing occurred. He smiled at me. His smile was warm and sincere. It took me by surprise. I looked away self consciously, fighting the urge to cower. As I looked back at Him, He was still looking at me and smiling approvingly. It seemed incredulous, yet this all-powerful, huge and threatening monarch was smiling upon me as if to assure me I had His approval. He liked me! Could it be true?

The scene continued. His approval was having a wonderful effect on me. Instead of withdrawing in fear from

His presence, I was compelled to approach Him. And this I did, slowly, to be sure. Yet with each hesitant step forward I felt more reassurance. His smile became more appealing. I was confident that moving toward Him was the right thing to do.

Suddenly I was aware of waves of peace washing over me. It was as if I was entering a place that was familiar, yet I had not visited in a very long time. I felt good. Contentment flooded my being. Peace flowed throughout my body, soothing my mind and caressing the deepest parts of my soul. The feelings of intimidation, vulnerability, and fear were gone! His approval and acceptance of me, in spite of all my uselessness, had transformed my fear into joy. I was insignificant without His approval. Yet, I had His approval. So, not only was I significant, I was loved. The most powerful authority in the universe loved me! The fearsome and magnificent God loved me!

The joy that flooded my soul was unfathomable. There are certainly no words to describe what I felt that night. This was truly the peace that surpasses man's ability to comprehend!

This is the awesome God that created the heavens and the Earth. He put the stars and planets in their places. He is the One who planted the Garden in Eden and placed the first man and woman there. He is the God that told Noah to build a huge boat in a place where rain had not fallen in years. This God caused Abram's barren one hundred-year-old wife to conceive a child. He is a miracle working God. There is nothing He cannot do, if He decides to do it. Whether that is to divide the waters of the Red Sea so three million people and their livestock can cross it on dry ground, or to drown an Egyptian army, horses, chariots, and all in the same sea, only hours later. He is the God of ALL flesh. That means He owns it all. There is nothing too difficult for Him. Nothing impossible. He started it all and He will end it when He wants to. And there is nothing anyone in heaven or on Earth can do to stop Him from doing what He wants, when He wants.

However, the most incredible thing is this: He loves you and I, just like we are! He has told us to call Him, Father. His various titles are; The Great I AM, The One True God, The God of Abraham, Isaac, and Jacob, and many more. But He said we, you and me, are to address Him as, Father. He wants us to know how much He loves us. He wants us to come to Him confidently with our problems, our pain, and our plans. He wants to shower us with His loving provision and keep us safe with His powerful protection. He is more than enough to handle any situation that arises. He delights in providing for us.

One particular story from our life with God illustrates this very well.

When Michele and I have an important decision to make, we pray and ask God to reveal His will for us in the situation. We learned a long time ago the benefit and joy found in doing things God's way. He definitely knows best. We have seen numerous times how wonderfully he provides for us over and above what we would have provided for ourselves in the same situation.

In this particular case, our dear friends, Chester and Betsy Kylstra invited us, to join them in their ministry as full time counselors. This meant relocating for the fifth time in ten years! Loading up the twenty-four foot Ryder again with all our personal belongings (can you spell dent and scratch?). It also meant explaining to our daughter, Lindsey, that God might be directing us to move, again!

More Than Enough

Not one of the three of us wanted to go through the ordeal of moving again. We liked where we were living. The beach was close. Lindsey had two new and good friends. And we wanted to put down roots, once and for all. Moving was not one of our immediate plans. Yet, we do teach and preach that to do God's will is always best. There were benefits in joining Chester and Betsy's ministry. We just wished they could move the ministry to us!

So, we talked. Lindsey was not interested. Michele wasn't either. But Michele and I have also learned that when we really are stumped and the decision is a biggie we must be agreement. We both must feel the same thing. At times we have even asked God for a sign, something to confirm the direction we feel He is leading us. In this case we asked Him for two things. First, if He wanted us to move again we asked Him to change our feelings toward moving. "Change our hearts and give us peace, Lord," we prayed. And number two; "Give us one thousand dollars to pay the cost of the move."

It was just before Christmas when the Kylstra's gave us the invitation. The first indication that God was on the move was when I was given an unexpected gift for Christmas. It was a check for nine hundred dollars! As I was driving home after being given the check I thought, "Well, we asked for one thousand, we only need one hundred more." When I arrived home I told Michele the good news. Her response was, "No, we asked for one thousand dollars. That's wonderful but it's only nine hundred." She went on to say that if God wanted us to go He would give us one thousand, because that's what we asked for, not nine hundred. She can be real firm when it comes to details. I responded, "Okay, okay. We asked for one thousand and that's what it'll take to get us out of here."

That night in my prayer time, I thanked God for the nine hundred. But, I reminded Him, "We did ask for one thousand."

A couple of days later, after Christmas and before New Year's Eve, a friend called and said they wanted to see us and asked if could they come by. We thought, "Oh, are they going to bring us the thousand?" Well, they didn't. But they did give us a check for five hundred dollars! We were very excited and thanked them profusely for their generosity. We now had fourteen hundred dollars. Michele reminded me again that we had asked for one thousand.

A couple more days passed and we got another call from some friends from out of town whom we had not seen in a couple of years. They wanted to drive up to see us and have lunch. They said they had a Christmas present for us and wanted to give it to us in person. To make a long and wonderful story short, they gave us a check for one thousand dollars! We were going to move.

Soon after their visit, fourteen-year-old Lindsey announced that she was ready to go. "Yep, I can go now," she announced confidently. Michele asked why she had changed her mind. Lindsey replied, "I didn't change my mind, God did." She said she had been praying as we had agreed to pray and God had changed her resistance to acceptance.

Before we moved, which we did in the third week in January, we were given another check for five hundred dollars. We had asked for one thousand. God had given the $900.00, $500.00 $1,000.00 $500.00. Total $2,900.00! And when we moved into our new home on the Lake overlooking the Gulf of Mexico we received another check for $580.00. Total given to confirm God's will for us to move; $3,480.00!

Our God is a big God and He does big things! Don't be afraid to draw close to Him. He will reassure you of His love for you. He will change your life for the better!

Epilogue

Sanctify them by Your truth. Your word is truth (John 17: 17).

As mentioned at the beginning of this book, these stories are true and happened as we have related them here. Our intention was to tell stories from our life that will encourage you to pursue your own life with God. We have concentrated on stories that illustrate practical ways God provided for us as we tried our best to find, follow, and fulfill His will for our lives, our marriage, and our ministry. Obviously, we have not shared all the exciting stories we could. There isn't room in this small volume and it isn't necessary. However, we have seen many similar and miraculous events in the lives of other people that have found a new life with God through their faith in Jesus Christ.

Many of the other stories we could tell we have had a direct part in. But due to the personal nature of them, those stories are best told by the people who have lived them. We know them because Michele and I have worked as counselors to the body of Christ since our conversion experience nearly twenty years ago. During the last twenty years we have counseled many hundreds of God's children from literally around the world. We have taught in churches and colleges. We have traveled throughout the United States counseling, and training church counselors. We currently correspond with dozens of people whom we have helped go on with their life with God. From them we continue to hear of the many wonderful ways God interacts with them as they faithfully follow His plan for their lives. We are truly blessed by the stories we hear that testify of God's goodness.

It is our sincerest prayer that these stories have encouraged you to know God personally. For there is a day coming, and soon, when we will see Him face to face. At that time the effectiveness of our lifestyle on this planet will become undeniably clear. Now is the time to review our lives, our purpose, and our plans for the future to make sure all of it glorifies God and helps others. Jesus said our love for God could not be separated from our love for our fellow man. He said if we loved Him we would love each other.

We are surrounded by an ungodly culture that pulls at us from every direction. In this, we are no different than Jesus and His first disciples. But we who have answered the call from God must show the people of the world His love. He commanded us to love them and He will empower us to do it. And if we don't, who will? And if we love them, we will because we know Him, love Him, and desire nothing more than to glorify Him with our words and actions.

May God, our Father, and our Lord Jesus bless you with the powerful presence of His Spirit as you pursue your life with Him.

Short Stories
by Mike Green

The Christmas Vision

Christmas morning is a very special time for most ten-year-old boys. It was certainly no different for me. I wakened with the anticipation that something good was about to happen. Thoughts of presents and toys and turkey dinner tumbled through my fuzzy head as I sat up in bed and rubbed the sleep from my eyes. If I had not tried to stay awake through the night I would not have slept as soundly as I had. I did my best to fight off sleep but in the end I couldn't maintain my vigil and drifted into deep sleep sometime after midnight. Now, as I sat in my bed and yawned hard and wide I tried to focus on the events that awaited me downstairs. Generally, Christmas is a great day. It's always filled with lots of fun and food and friends and family. And most of the time the toys were great! But there was one thing that bothered me.

Even though previous Christmases had been wonderful I was always left with the sense that one special gift was not there. Christmas after Christmas it was the same; there were plenty of really cool toys to play with for a while but, something special was missing. I never complained though, and instead tried to act grateful for the gifts I did receive. But there was always that nagging emptiness which all the festive celebration and the new toys just didn't seem to fill. As I pulled on my jeans and slipped my tee shirt over my head I wondered if this was the year things would be different. I hurriedly shoved my feet into my high tops as my excitement grew. I smiled and thought to myself, "Maybe this is the year."

The hallway that led to the stairs was dark as my parents continued to sleep soundly in their room at the end of the hall. The only lights on downstairs were the Christmas decorations my dad strung with such patience every year. I ran to the top of the stairs and stopped for a moment to gaze in awe at the shimmering colored lights lining the wide doorway into the family room. The French doors were left open and invited me like outstretched arms into the treasure room below. The family room was filled with the glittering decorations and twinkling lights and piles of presents that made this holiday the best one of the year. I leaned down on the railing resting my chin on my hands and stared wide-eyed at the exciting scene below me. Silently I hoped this was the year it would happen.

I walked slowly down the stairs as the first rays of dawn began to light up the morning. The warm glow of dawn crept into the house and competed with the Christmas lights for my attention. This was truly a beautiful morning. I smiled broadly and walked slowly into the family room. It felt like I was entering the great hall of a powerful king. The room was aglow with the sparkling lights shimmering red and gold and green and white. Their brilliance surpassed the lights of any other Christmas. They seemed brighter, clearer, more intense and even more inviting than usual. It was as if they were alive. Though the house was still, without a sound, the hundreds of lights on the tall stately Christmas tree seemed to sing. The room was filled with the fresh fragrance of pine.

Every year my father always selected a terrific tree. He had a knack for finding the right one. And every year I was thrilled when the day finally arrived and we drove out into the country to view the trees. One of the highlights of Christmas

The Christmas Vision

Eve was lighting the beautiful tree standing in the family room. But this year my father had out done himself. The tree was magnificent! It took all the self- control I could muster to contain my excitement. I felt like a TV cowboy reigning in the team of high-spirited horses hitched to his wagon. Only my team was pounding their impatient hooves in the dusty street of my heart. I was trying my best to take it all in and to make this moment last a little longer. My little heart was beating wildly under my tee shirt. My breath seemed to leave me. I felt like I was going to faint under the weight of the beauty that enveloped me. My feelings had become a perplexing mixture of uncontrollable excitement and sublime peace. I wanted to stand still and run away at the same time. I stood silent, mesmerized by the incredible spectacle that danced around me.

Then I noticed the present under the tree. It was one among many competing for my attention. But it was different than the others in some way. It shined with a special brilliance that captivated me, drawing me to itself like iron shavings to a magnet. I walked immediately over to it. Reaching into the pile I picked up the present marveling at the unique wrapping paper. I held the present in my shaking hands and stared at it. All of a sudden I regained my wits and realized I was holding a Christmas present! What was I thinking?

Instantly I began to tear the paper away from the box, clawing at it like only a ten-year- old boy can do on Christmas morning. As I removed the paper I saw the label on the box and oh how my heart leapt with joy! Could it be? Could it really be that it was finally here? With trembling hands and racing breath, I lifted the lid of the box and saw it. Oh my! Oh my! I fumbled for words, trying to speak something that would do justice to the magnificence of my gift. But every attempt to voice my excitement offered nothing more intelligible than mumbles and slurred ooh's and ah's. Pulling the precious gift

Life with God

from the box I stood for a moment reveling in pure joy! Then, turning toward the door that opened onto our front yard, I ran to it and pulling it aside, I launched myself out into the clear morning air. "Yes!" This is it!" I sang as I danced across the lawn.

Time slipped away as I lost myself in the company of my new gift. An hour or so after leaving the house I heard my father call me from the front porch.

"Good morning, son! Merry Christmas!" He waved and smiled warmly.

I turned and ran toward the house and the wonderful man standing at the top of the steps.

"Good morning, daddy, and merry Christmas to you!" I called.

Before I could say another word he spoke, "I see you found your present."

"Yes, I did and thank you, thank you. It is just what I wanted."

"Well good, I'm glad you like it."

"Oh, I do. I do. I love it! It's so beautiful!"

"Well, I'm happy you're happy with it. But there are more presents under the tree for you."
"Oh, no. I have what I want. I mean," I stuttered, "this is too much. It's everything and more than I expected it would be."

The Christmas Vision

Again he said, "Well good I'm glad you like it so much. But there are more in here with your name on them."

AI know and, well, thank you," I said bursting with gratitude. "But, really this is all I want."

I thought I heard a touch of sadness in his voice when he replied, "Well, okay. If you're happy, that's what I want. But there are more, lots more, when you're ready." And saying that, he turned and walked back into the house, closing the door behind him. I was left standing in the yard holding my new treasure in my hands.

As I slowly regained my senses I realized I had just seen a vision. It seemed so real though. Was it a vision, really? I wasn't sleeping, so it could not have been a dream. No, it was a vision. Slowly, I began to separate real life from the vision of Christmas I just had experienced. It had been one of those open eyed visions where you're still awake but you lose track of time and space for just a moment, maybe even just a split second.

The Christmas vision was pleasant, much like a dream. I had no sense that anything supernatural was taking place. When it was over I didn't think too hard about it, I just went on with my business. But after two or three days I was still thinking about it. I believe when God reveals something to me, He does so for a reason. So, a few days later in prayer I asked the Holy Spirit for more information. "What was that about?"

This is what I believe I heard Holy Spirit say, "The Father speaks many times to His children through dreams and visions. That's what you experienced. It was a vision. People tend to remember information longer when it is given in a dream or vision. It has more impact.

"I'll say it does." I replied honestly.

"The gift in the vision is your salvation." He went on, "that's why you were so excited about it. It is the very best gift anyone can receive. Its value cannot be fully understood by any man until the moment he sees heaven, and his Heavenly Father for the first time. Then he understands the value of salvation, the seriousness of sin, and the incomparable sacrifice the Son made at the Cross."

"In the vision," I replied, "I did not want the other gifts under the tree. I saw them, they had my name on them. But compared to the first gift they were of no interest to me. What were they?"

His Spirit spoke again, "They represent all the other gifts your Heavenly Father has for you. Without doubt, salvation is the best gift for it changes your life eternally, which cannot be understood until you pass from this physical life into the spiritual life. But salvation contains the blessings of many more gifts as well. Your Father has many, many gifts for His children. Remember, you are a joint heir with Jesus Christ. Because you share His death, through conviction and repentance, and baptism, you may also share His life, His authority, and His wealth. Remember, your Father wants to conform you to the image of His Son."

"Why didn't I want those other gifts, then?" I asked.
"The Heavenly Father's children turn down His gifts for a variety of reasons. It is very sad. One very common reason is ignorance."

"What do you mean, ignorance?" I asked.

"His children do not realize the abundance He has for them. They are introduced to Him through their conversion experience, but too often they do not want to know Him. They have salvation and are satisfied. This attitude is the reason so many of His children attend weekly religious meetings but have no ongoing daily relationship with me. But, you may remember, the Father was not pleased with that attitude when the children of Israel embraced it. He spoke of it through the prophet Isaiah."

"Another common reason His children disregard the other gifts is because of arrogance. They want the benefits of His death but do not want to embrace His lifestyle. When they consider all they must give up to embrace the other gifts they instead want too pursue their own fun or fame. However, fulfilling your will can never produce for you the pleasure and peace that pursuing God's will produces."

"And some of His children reject the concept of additional gifts because they are lazy. They realize if they are to have more they must read the Word more, resist sin more, and believe the Father's promises in spite of circumstances that testify to the contrary. They think it's easier to take life as it comes than to do the work of praying, studying, serving, and growing, all of which is required for living a full life in Him. After salvation, unless one renews his thought process by taking every thought captive to the obedience of Christ, his behavior stays much as it was before he met the Savior. Unless he allows me to transform him by the renewing of his mind so that he can embrace the mind of Christ, he continues to think, act, and speak from the foundation of his former unredeemed mind. He may be saved but his life does not reflect his new condition. It is unfortunate.

"And finally, many of the Father's children do not feel worthy to receive anything good from Him. Their early childhood experience has taught them they are worthless, useless, and undeserving of having anything but trials, struggles, and pain. Even after they are reborn they never truly see themselves as the Lord sees them, that is, as His children, with all the rights, privileges, and honor their new birth has bestowed upon them.

"However, truly there is no end to the gifts that your Heavenly Father has for you, here and now, as well as there and then. Jesus said this."

I continued to listen as He continued to speak.

"Many of His children say they are hungry for more of God. They pray and say they want more love, more power, and more of God in their life. But they do not act like they want more. What is the reason for this? It's because they do not know what hunger is. They have never been hungry. Have you ever been hungry?"

"Well, no I guess, really truly hungry, no, I have not been hungry." I answered honestly.

"It's true. You have never missed a meal. You have fasted many meals. You have fasted many days at one time. And that is a good thing to do from time to time to clear your body and your mind so you can have a special time of prayer. But you have never missed a meal because you had nothing to eat. You have never been desperate for your next meal. You have never felt as if you were going to die if you did not eat. Have you?"

Again, I answered, "No."

He went on, "If you have not known hunger, then what do you mean when you say you are hungry for more of God?"

The Christmas Vision

A I don't know, maybe I can't say it. Maybe I'm not really hungry." I offered weakly.

The Holy Spirit continued. "Hungry men are desperate men. They will do anything to eat, including stealing. If they are desperate enough they will even kill, to get something to eat. If one is hungry for more of God, he will demonstrate that hunger by the amount of time he spends in prayer. Being hungry implies being depleted and needing to be refilled. Remember, the Word says, " the fervent" prayer of a righteous man gets results. It is because the desperate man will settle for nothing short of what he wants. He will pray as if his life depended on getting the answer. When you pray with such intensity you are indeed praying like a hungry man. Your heavenly Father enjoys hearing and responding to the prayers of hungry men"

My response to this vision is; "Teach me to be hungry, Lord."

Where are you in all of this? What does it mean to you when the Lord speaks of hunger? Are you hungry for more of God in your life? Are you desperate to see the manifestations of God's peace and power in your life? I believe if you are then you are probably seeing those manifestations. And you will continue to see them and they will increase.

The Tree and the Bird

Once upon a time there was a forest that stood on a bluff overlooking the sea. There were many different varieties of trees inhabiting the forest. Some were very old and very tall and straight. They reached up so high as if to touch the clouds floating above their waving tops. The soaring birds enjoyed relaxing in the loftiest branches of the trees. While the birds rested after each of their soaring adventures, they smiled happily as the fresh sea breeze caressed their feathers. The birds looked out across the endless expanse of sea and marveled at the beauty of their world.

Other trees had broad trunks with branches that stretched out wide in all directions. They grew close to the ground. They provided homes for the rabbits and squirrels in the rich soil at the base of their trunks. The singing birds perched in the tree's branches serenading the other animals with their beautiful songs.

As the trees stood erect on the bluff, breathing in the salt air carried on the sea breeze, they whispered among themselves how good it was to know the Father had place them there. They took pride in knowing the Father had designed them to provide homes and shelter and nourishment for the animals that lived among them. They had purpose. They felt useful. They were content.

The Father sent rain and sunshine, each in it's turn, to help the trees grow. The rain soaked the ground and sent their cool refreshing water to their roots. It rinsed their branches and made their leaves shine. The sun would then sparkle in the deep green hues of their leaves, dancing off the droplets that decorated the trees after the rain.

II

One day a storm approached the bluff from far out over the sea. The clouds gathered together in ever-tighter formations. They turned from their usual white to gray and then to black in a very short time. The trees looked out over the sea and knew this was to be a more violent storm than any they had seen before. They shuddered with anticipation and braced themselves as the first strong gusts of wind reached the foot of the bluff. The force of the wind increased rapidly. The younger trees looked to the older ones for reassurance. "Have courage, little brothers," the old ones replied confidently.

The wind whipped across the surface of the sea and quickly transformed the quiet ripples into frothing waves. The waves then crashed against the bluff splashing up higher and higher. As the water ran back to the sea it etched gullies into the face of the bluff. The storm came closer and continued to gather strength.

The young trees were frightened and cried out to their larger brothers, "What shall we do?" The wise trees responded calmly, "Stand strong and have courage. The Father knows of this storm. It does not come as a surprise to Him. If He allows it, it has a purpose. He uses everything for a good purpose. He can be trusted to care for us, even during the storm." But the small trees had never seen the wind blow with such fury. They wanted to believe the older trees but they remained afraid.

The Tree and the Bird

Suddenly great peals of thunder began to roll through the heavens. The ground on the bluff shook. Lightening cracked the sky under the hideous black clouds. Its menacing white-hot tentacles threatened to ignite the branches of the tallest trees. The birds took cover in the thickest branches. They huddled together and turned their beaks to their backs. They tucked their heads under their wings and gripped the branches as hard as they could with their clawed feet. The rabbits and squirrels frantically scurried to safety inside their homes at the base of the trees.

The air temperature cooled dramatically as the first giant drops of rain began to fall. At first the raindrops were singular and cool. They splattered refreshingly as they hit the trees. But as the wind increased the raindrops began to sting the trees. Soon the drops were so close together and falling so heavily that they became indistinguishable from one another. The rain was driven harshly by the howling wind. It was as though the sky had turned to liquid and was breaking apart. From the highest heaven the clouds threw the rain down upon the earth in great torrents. Lightening flashed angrily and the roar of the thunder shook the trees.

One particular young tree was very frightened. He had never experienced such demonized fury! It seemed as though the Father had lost control of the sky. The ground shook under his roots and he was afraid he would lose his hold in the soil. The wind whipped his branches until he knew they would be ripped out of their sockets in his trunk. His leaves were torn from his branches as the furious wind screamed through the forest. His trunk began to tremble wildly and his roots slipped in the wet soil. "Oh no!" he thought, "I can't hold on!" He felt his roots let go as another angry gust of wind slammed into him.

It the next instant he was down in the mud, lying on his branches. Suspended over the bluff at a sickening angle the weight of his branches was too much for him to hold. His roots finally snapped and he tumbled wildly down the bluff and into the sea.

III

The young tree braced himself to meet the crash of the waves. He hit the cold water hard with a painful splash. Once in the sea, he was bashed against the shore of the bluff. Wave after wave threw him against the muddy bank. He wondered if his end had come. "How can I survive this beating?" he thought as he repeatedly crashed into the bluff. "I am a tree," he said to himself, "and trees are not designed to be ripped from the ground and thrown into the sea." Despair swept over him as he was attacked by the boiling waves of the sea.

Slowly the current carried the wounded tree away from the shore of the bluff. He bobbed on the surface of the sea as the rain continued to beat down upon his torn branches and ripped bark. He looked to the heavens trying to find some sign that the storm was abating. But the rain poured down from the dark clouds and the thunder rolled and the wind beat the sea into a seething white rage. The tree felt lost and without hope. He was at the mercy of the elements. He had been ruthlessly stripped of all traces of the wonderful life he had known in the forest on the bluff. Confusion clouded his thoughts as he tried to find a reason for the frightening events. "Why is this happening to me?" he asked himself, "Where is the father?" Over and over he asked.

As each wave lifted him to it's crest, he could see the forest. It grew smaller and smaller drifting away in the distance. Through the mist of rain and the spray from the waves he could tell he was moving further out into the sea. His heart sank deeper as each wave lifted beneath him. He was adrift on the cruel sea. Separated from his destiny. A tree floating in the ocean. "What will become of me?" he cried out to the wind and waves. But they did not answer his desperate plea. And he drifted on, moving further and further away from his home.

IV

As the tree drifted on at the mercy of the current, the wind began to ease. The crests of the waves grew less ragged. Their tops were no longer being blown off in great puffs of white spray. The rain slowed down to drizzle as the clouds began to break apart giving up their dark color. The thunder and lightening disappeared. The tree was relieved. As he was raised to the tops of the waves he could no longer see the bluff. The tallest trees had long since dropped behind the curve of the horizon. He was completely alone, first rising upon the backs of the mountainous waves only to quickly sink again into their cavernous valleys.

"What will become of me?" the tree asked again. He had been designed by the Father to dwell in the forest and to provide shelter and nourishment for the animals. That was his role in the play of life on earth. Adrift on the sea he would no longer have the simple pleasure of doing what he was created to do. He was without purpose, bobbing on the waves of the sea. His torn bark hurt and his wounded heart ached. The salt of the seawater brought stinging pain to his sores. His once elegant branches hung uselessly from his trunk, broken off as he was carried out into the deepest part of the unknown expanse of sea. He was useless, and hopeless. He was helplessly destined to drift at the whim of the wind and current.

Days passed slowly. The sun beat down on the floating tree and the sky was filled with the white puffy clouds of peace. The waves had grown quiet and the surface of the sea

Life with God

was smooth and calm. The sky and clouds reflected in the mirrored green surface of the sea. The world had returned to normal. Stars filled the night sky to shimmer and twinkle like diamonds. The tree found his greatest pleasure during the cool evenings gazing into the dark sky as he drifted.

He had resigned himself to his new life in the sea. He knew he could not change his condition or his position. He had no better choice but to try to make the best of whatever came his way. In the first few days after the storm he struggled to find some reason to explain his sad condition. But eventually he gave up. He thought, "What difference does it make, I can't change it?" However, one thing still bothered him. He could not forget what the wise tree had told him many times about the Father. "He uses everything a good reason." He had said it with such confidence. At first, the younger tree tried to believe there was truth in the wise one's statement. However, since being cast into the sea he no longer believed the wise one's remarks. He even began to doubt the existence of the Father. Though from time to time, the words of the wise one still echoed through his memories.

V

Then one day as the tree was drifting he saw something in the sky way off in the distance. At first he couldn't believe it. He strained to see if it really was there. He watched the thing closely. It seemed to be moving in the sky. "Is it a bird?" he asked himself. His heart leaped at the thought that he might not be alone. As he strained to see clearly he realized, for the first time since he was so mercilessly ripped from his home he was looking at another living thing. "Can it be true?" he wondered hopefully.

As he watched, the tree noticed the bird was flying toward him. He hoped he was not betrayed by his sight. He studied the bird carefully. "Yes! It is flying this way!" he said with

The Tree and the Bird

delight. Looking intently at the bird the tree observed that his wings flapped awkwardly. He didn't soar like the birds that lived in the tall trees on the bluff. His flying was more laborious. His wings didn't move in the short swift strokes of the songbirds either. Yet, he did not resemble the sea birds that swirled in the updrafts at the edge of the bluff. "What kind of bird is this?" he thought.

As the bird came closer the tree realized that he was struggling to stay in the air. With each flap of his wings he was sinking lower in the sky. He was getting closer to the tree but he was also getting dangerously close to the surface of the sea. "He is hurt," the tree remarked aloud.

The bird approached even closer and the tree could see pain in the bird's eyes. He ached for the bird as he was immediately reminded of the pain he suffered when he was torn from the bluff by the storm. Thoughts of that overwhelming pain flooded his memory as he watched the bird's difficult flight. He winced inwardly each time the bird's wounded wings split the air. He knew that, as he himself had done during the storm, the bird was fighting for his life.

By the time the bird finally reached the floating tree, he was only inches above the water. Hovering briefly, he slowly descended and gently dropped to the trunk of the tree. At first he stood motionless, gasping. His chest heaved as he tried to recover from this difficult flight. He glanced cautiously at the tree, and then at the water of the sea, making sure he was safe. Then he readjusted his wings with a flutter and tucked them against his sides. He was completely exhausted. Yet there was also a look of thankful relief on his smooth elegant face. When he had reassured himself that he was safely perched on the trunk of the floating tree he lowered his beak against his breast, closed his eyes, and fell into a deep sleep.

The tree watched the bird admiringly. "How truly beautiful he is," the tree thought to himself. "I wonder what he is doing out here in the middle of the vast expanse of sea?" A brief uninvited thought of the Father flashed in his mind. He quickly pushed it aside, and concentrated on the bird. "He is tired and perhaps wounded," he thought. "A bird would have to fly a long way to be so exhausted and to fall asleep so fast. It is a good thing for him I was here." The words of the wise tree crowded again into his thoughts, "The Father uses everything for a good reason. He pondered the words as they echoed again and again.

As the tree listened again to the wise trees words he felt something bubbling up from within himself. He tried to hold it back, to swallow it. But, it felt too good. He hadn't felt it since he left the bluff overlooking the sea. So, he relaxed and let the feeling come to the surface. In an instant, he knew what it was. Once again he had a purpose. Even though he no longer dwelled in the forest, he was still useful. The wise one was right. The Father was real and He had chosen to use the tree in a way the tree would never have imagined! The bird was safe. The Father could be trusted. The tree sighed contentedly as a tear of thanksgiving fell into the sea. And from that day to this, trees continue to drift quietly across the vast expanse of sea, carried on by the current, fulfilling the Father's plan for their lives, in ways they never would have imagined.

The End

The Man, the Mountain and God

Once upon a time a man set out to climb to the top of a mountain. It was not a particularly high mountain. Nor was it too dangerous for experienced climbers, like him. It was, however, a mountain that he had never climbed before.

Before beginning his ascent he studied the mountain from his vantage point in the valley. As far as he could see there were no major obstacles along his proposed route. He thought this outing would be more like a casual hike than a difficult climb. As he packed his gear, he reasoned his trek to the summit would take him less than half a day. He would then have lunch and return to the valley before dark. So, he packed light, taking only the essentials required for a one-day hike.

As dawn stretched its earliest golden rays across the eastern sky, the man began his ascent. The walk was easy and he made good time. The morning sun climbed with him, moving higher into the sky as he moved higher up the mountain. He was showered with bird songs from the trees and a small stream gurgled along side him from time to time. He considered as he walked how fortunate he was to witness the glorious beauty of God's creation.

At one point he stopped to admire the view and to drink from the little stream. The water was cold and exhilarating as it slid down into his body, refreshing his muscles. He sat still on an outcropping of rock letting his booted feet dangle over the precipice. Below he could see his starting point in the valley and the rolling foothills unfolding away to the horizon. He marveled at the magnificent vista God had prepared for him that day! As he looked out over the valley, drinking in the beauty before him, he was moved to worship God.

"Oh, how grand and glorious you are, Father! You are mighty and awesome, beyond my ability to comprehend! And to think you, the originator of all life would look upon me with favor and lavish your grace upon me! It is almost too good to believe!" He sat in silence as the love and peace of God's presence washed over him.

Time slipped by slowly as he sat and worshipped. But then he remembered his quest and stirred himself to action. He knew he had spent more time idle than he planned. He scolded himself for his losing track of time and determinedly resumed his climb.

He climbed steadily throughout the remaining morning hours and reached the top of the mountain not too far behind his schedule. He was happy with his progress and rejoiced! The climb had exhilarated him. The time with God had inspired him. And he was thrilled to have reached his objective on time in spite of his delay.

The man found a spot under the overhang of a large rock and sat down to have his lunch before beginning his descent. Leaning back against the cool rock he opened his backpack and ate his lunch. He was surrounded by peace. The wind blew lightly across the mountaintop. The sun shone down on his bare legs and arms and face. "Hmmmm." He smiled,

"What a thrill it is to meet with you like this, Lord." As he rested, digesting his lunch, he thought of God, and sleep overcame him. He slept and dreamed of God. He was with God, together in heaven, finally! It was more beautiful than he had ever

The streets of gold glittered radiantly. The voices of worshiping millions sang endless praise. The omnipresent light of God's glory illuminated everything and everywhere at once!

"So this is it. I am really here! I can't believe it!" he remarked with delight. Scene after glorious scene passed before him as if he were watching a movie at the cinema. Overwhelmed by the beauty of his New World, he pinched himself to make sure it wasn't a dream.

"Ouch!" he screamed. And he awoke with a fright. "Oh, it was a dream." The man was saddened at the realization. He sat rubbing the sore spot on his arm where he had pinched himself. He shook his head and chuckled at his foolishness. Then he stood and stretched. The mid-afternoon sun shone bright through the white clouds that drifted across the blue sky.

Realizing he had slept too long he anxiously repacked his gear. A shiver of fear quickly flashed through his mind. "I must get started in order to reach the valley before dark," the man said out loud to himself. He grabbed his hiking stick and started to retrace his steps back down the mountain. He stepped lively and quickened his pace. Knowing he must get down before dark he was agitated that he had wasted so much time dreaming. Down and down he went. In and out of the sun, through the trees. Small pebbles scattered before him as his boots struck the earth with purpose.

As he made his way down the mountain, the sun crept steadily across the sky to the west. Seeking a destination beyond the horizon it now seemed to race against him. He began to think of it as his opponent. Locked in the spirit of competition he raced to finish the contest ahead of the sun. As another hour ticked by he began to realize he was not going to beat the sun. He grew more anxious with each passing moment. It was as though the clock was ticking against him. The impending darkness grew closer with each beat of his anxious heart.

At the same time his climbing experience told him to slow his gait. He was moving too quickly to remain sure-footed on the downhill grade. But he wanted to beat the sun. He did not want to spend the night on the mountain. He was not equipped for it. The mountains were dangerous after dark.

On he went, down, down. As the afternoon light began to fade he knew he had lost his race against the sun. He wasn't going to enter the valley before dark. This angered him. Again he quickened his pace. His heart raced and he forced the cool air of early evening into his lungs.

Then, just after the last glow of sunset faded away, it happened! As the trail twisted through the trees, he lost his footing in the loose gravel and failed to regain his balance. Down he went onto his back. He was moving so rapidly when he fell that he could not stop himself. He tumbled away from the path over and over, first head over heels, then sideways. Spinning down he bumped and crashed through small trees and shrubs. The saplings stung him and briars pulled at his clothes and pricked his skin as he rolled. He tried to stop himself but could not. He lost track of up and down. Then he was weightless and falling through the night air! Though it was only for a second or two it seemed like time stopped. Yet, no sooner was he launched into the air than he slammed into solid rock. Stunned by the impact he grabbed at the surface of the rock. He was sickened to feel how vertical the face of the rock was. His fingers tried to dig into the rock. Instead the tips of his fingers were ripped by the rough surface and began to bleed. His numbed mind raced with fear as he slid down to what he knew was his death.

As his life began to pass before him, his right hand smashed against and automatically wrapped around a root the size of a small child's wrist growing out of a crack in the rock! He clutched the root with all his strength and his descent into death stopped instantly.

He hung suspended from the root gasping for breath like a dying fish from an angler's hook. His hand ached as his vice like grip strangled the small fibrous chord sticking out of the rock. But the tumbling had stopped. He was relieved. His arm ached. He felt sure it was broken from the weight of his body being stopped so abruptly against the root. Fire ran from the palm of his hand to the top of his shoulder. Oh, how he ached! But he was no longer tumbling out of control. He had stopped. His arm and hand cried for mercy, but he was not about to let their complaints force him to release his hold on the root. He hung motionless, his cheek pressed against the cool rock, like a slab of butchered meat drying in the market stall.

His breathing came in great gulps. He was more frightened than he had ever been. Every bone and muscle in his body screamed for release from the torture. But he held fast to his root of life. Slowly his breathing began to return to normal. He took a mental inventory of the pain in each muscle, each joint, and each bone. He could not remember a time when he hurt so much.

With all his remaining strength he reached up with his free hand and grabbed the root. With both hands he tried to pull himself up into a more comfortable position. The pain was unbearable. Slowly he straightened his arms again.

"How long can I hang here?" he thought to himself. He hung quietly, thinking. "What can I do? Why must it be so dark?" The helplessness of his situation swarmed over him like a storm cloud. There was no escape. "I'm trapped, hung out here hopeless and doomed." He remained perfectly still, hearing only the relentless drumming of his heart and feeling the searing pain in his arms and hands.

Suddenly out of the stillness, a voice addressed him.

"Let go."

At first he ignored it. Then it called again. Quietly, comfortingly, "Let go."

His first thought was that the voice was a pain-induced death wish. "No," he spoke aloud. "No, I'm not going to let go. I'll work something out." He determined to hold on as long as he could.

Minutes turned into hours. Each one filled with intensifying pain and despair.

The man thought, "Maybe I can hang here until the light of morning comes. But how long is that?" He grimaced with pain as a bolt of fire shot through his arm.

Another hour filled with unbearable pain passed slowly. "Let go," the voice whispered again. "Let go."

This time he responded to the voice in anger. "Oh, sure," he screamed. "Just let go and be smashed to death like a bug under my boot. No thank you. I won't! I can't!" He stifled tears of desperation, determined more than ever to hold onto the root. But the voice came again, calm yet insistent.

"Trust me, and let go."

The man's hands slipped an inch or two on the root. He tried to reposition his grip, but knew it was pointless. He could not hold onto the root indefinitely. His hands ached. His arms had become numb. He began to whimper like a scolded child.

He felt the soft caress of a strong yet tender hand on his cheek wiping away his bloodstained tears. It reminded him of a time long ago during his childhood when his father would hold him tenderly in his powerful arms while he rocked him to sleep. During those quiet times all the pain and confusion of his troubled little world would melt away like winter snow in the warm sunlight of spring. Free of his hurts he would sigh contentedly and drift down into the silent peace of deep sleep.

As he revisited those wonderful experiences snuggled in his father's love, a smile crept across the man's anguished face. A barely audible sigh escaped his lips as if inviting another caress. The next caress touched his deepest pain. Hanging there upon the rock, exposed to the night air, his confusion eased. No longer the life saving anchor of hope, he saw the root as the chains of death, preventing him from tasting life's richest pleasure. There was only one thing to do. His hands relaxed, the root slipped from his grasp, and he fell into the outstretched arms of God.

The End

The Silver Cup

I

Once upon a time in a war torn land far away there lived a peculiar young man. The land he lived in had been in turmoil for as long as anyone could remember. There had been an ongoing feud between those who believed in the God of the Elders and those who believed in numerous Other gods. This feud greatly disturbed the young man. His peculiarity was a result of his strong desire to help end the feud. Yet throughout the years many of war the Elders had attempted to negotiate with the others. But they did not succeed.

Like his family for generations before him, the young man was a follower of the God of the elder's. Since he had been a very young boy he had listened to the elders tell stories of their God who was bigger than everything in the world. "God," they said, "is so big that He created the world and everything in it." They told him there was nothing the young man could know or learn that God didn't already know. There was no place in the world so remote that God had not already been there.

Often he would go to the river to be alone and sit and think of God. "If I could know God, and not just hear His story," the young man would say, "He could tell me how to help bring an end to the feuding." When he mentioned this to the elders, they would chuckle at his childish desire and reply,

Life with God

"No one knows God personally anymore, son. That only happened in the olden days when the sages lived in caves. Now we just read His story to learn about Him." This did not satisfy the young man and on occasion he would attempt to question the absurdity of such thinking.

Sitting with the elders in the evening before bed he would ask, "If there was a time when men knew God, and God told them His story, so they could tell us, and He was kind and loving, as you say, then why would He stop speaking to men?" Their reply was simple. "He just decided that He had said enough, and He stopped speaking." The young man's curiosity was not satisfied by this reasoning, and he would ask, "But, who said God just decided to quit speaking?"

"We no longer hear from Him. It's been years since the elders spoke with God," they would answer.

"But if God chose to speak He would, nothing could stop Him. After all, He's God." If the young man persisted with more questions, the elders would go on to explain, "God is loving and kind. He has made everything in the world for our enjoyment. Our responsibility is to live peacefully, work diligently, repeat our thanksgiving prayers daily, and share God's story with others who do not believe He exists. Sometimes they believe us and sometimes they don't. But we can't help that."

Although their explanations did not answer his questions, the young man was careful not to press the elders too far for fear of being disrespectful. But he really believed that the God of the Elders would want to speak to men. "Why wouldn't He?" he would often ask himself as he withdrew from the elders' presence.

The Silver Cup

One summer night, after he had discussed God with the elders, the young man went to bed more confused than ever before. His sleep was fitful and he tossed and turned on his straw filled mattress. After several hours of this unrest he was still wide-awake. He got up from his bed and walked to the door of his home. Looking out into the night sky he marveled at the brightness of the stars. "He has placed them there. All of them!" he said.

The stars appeared to be millions of twinkling diamonds scattered across an endless black sea. The young man was awe struck by the thought that God was big enough and wise enough to create such a wonderful spectacle. His desire to know this awesome God created in him a thirst for which he could find no satisfying drink. As he stared at the stars, he felt parched. It was as though he was dying of thirst. But he knew this thirst could not be quenched by water from the jug sitting on the small table beside his bed. Frustrated with his insatiable thirst the young man returned to his bed to wrestle with his thoughts of God until sleep finally rescued him.

II

The following morning the young man set off early to his work in the field. He looked forward to the hard labor of gathering vegetables. The heat of summer would keep his mind off thoughts of God. As he entered the field his co-workers met him. He also saw another young man he had never seen before.

"Good morning," the young man offered.

"Hello," was the reply.

"Are you going to be working with us today?" he asked the new man.

"Yes," the new man answered.

"Well, good, I can use the help."

The two men selected baskets from the stack beside the barn and walked out into the field together to begin searching through the green foliage for ripe vegetables. They talked as they worked side by side. It was soon obvious that one was a follower of the God of the Elder's and the other was not a follower of any god. Eventually, the unbeliever said he thought the young man's God was the product of the elder's fanciful thoughts.

"Purely fictitious," he said. "All this just happened. Who knows how or why and who cares? And why should I care? I'm just out here trying to get enough to eat and have a good time. And I'm doing pretty good at it too!"

"But, there is a God and He is good. He is the one who planned all this good. And he did it because he loves us," the young man offered kindly.

"Aw, you can believe it if it makes you feel good. But, I don't. What did your God do for you that was so good?" the unbeliever challenged.

"Well, he did a lot of good things," he responded. " Just look around you."

"Yeah, okay. I look around every day and all I see is people fighting over gods, I feel dissatisfied and hungry, and I have to work hard for food."

The young man never thought of it like that before. His life certainly didn't seem to be that way. He lived a good life.

He ate well. He slept comfortably. And he surely did not engage in fighting over gods! He wished the fighting would stop, but he didn't know how to stop it.

"Well maybe if you did follow the God of the Elders, your life would be better," he offered.

"Better than what? Look, I do what I want when I want. I don't need anyone to tell me what to do. No one. Not you, or your God, or anybody else. I like it that way. Now, why don't you shut up and let me work in peace and quiet?" And saying that the new man turned away and resumed his work of picking vegetables.

The young man was angry at the unbeliever's response. "How dare him say my God does not exist! I know he does." But as they worked in silence he thought about what the unbeliever had said.

Is God really a product of the elder's fanciful thoughts? How do they know God other than by the stories they read about Him? They haven't seen Him and they don't hear from Him anymore. Could it be true that He doesn't exist?" The young man's mind reeled at the thought of God's story being a fable. He felt nauseous and dizzy.

The unbeliever noticed his distress and asked, "Hey, what's wrong with you? You gonna be sick or somethin'?" The young man couldn't answer. He had grown weak at the thought that the God of the Elders might not be real.

Hey, you," the man called again, "you're white as a sheet."

The young man turned from the row of vegetables he had been working and stumbled through the other rows toward the edge of the field. He felt trapped and needed to escape. The question kept echoing in his head, "What if its all a fable?" Once clear of the last row of vegetables, he began to run down the dusty road toward the river. "God is not real," he thought as he ran. His face was soon drenched with perspiration, and his breathing grew labored. Within moments he was crashing through familiar bushes and shrubs near the river. As he ran, the taller trees of the river forest soon replaced the shrubs.

Once inside the forest he slowed his pace and began to walk. His breathing returned to normal and his face began to cool. He found his favorite rock and crawled up on it to sit and watch the river. The first thing he noticed was his thirst. This time he knew it was from running through the summer heat, not from his desire for God. He leaned down over the edge of the rock to scoop up some water in his hand. As he did he saw something shinning up from the bottom of the river. He sipped the cool water from his hand while staring at the shiny object beneath the surface.

When he had refreshed himself, he slipped off the rock and into the cool river. The water swirled around his knees. He put his face as close as possible to the water, felt for the object with his hand, and grasped it on the first try, removing it from where it had been lodged between two rocks. He then stood erect with water dripping from his hands and arms and looked at the small silver cup he had retrieved. Clutching the cup in his hand he climbed out of the river and back onto the rock.

III

The cup was not large or fancy. It was made of silver and had a tooled handle that resembled a flowering vine. The rim was round and smooth. The young man was immediately taken by the cup's simple elegance. He turned it, first one way then another, looking at it from all angles. He then rubbed it

The Silver Cup

dry with the dry part of his shirt and smiling, he set it down beside him on the rock. Finding the cup had brightened his mood.

The young man lay down with his back against the warm rock to let the summer sun dry him too. As he laid on the rock dozing in the warm sunlight his thoughts soon turned again to God.

He thought, " If God exists, I believe He would want to reveal himself to me." The young man then fell fast asleep.

While he slept he dreamed about the silver cup. In the dream he was walking through the streets of the town where the followers of other gods lived. The silver cup dangled from his belt. As he walked he saw people who were fat and satisfied from rich eating and heavy drinking. They seemed much taller than him and looked upon him with scorn. Others appeared to be parched with thirst and emaciated from lack of food. They were lean and haggard and looked at him with desperation in their eyes. Others didn't look at him at all, choosing instead to ignore him completely. To them he simply didn't exist.

The staring people frightened him. The fat ones made him feel self conscious and bothersome. Their faces showed contempt and seemed to say, "Away from me you worthless beggar!" Or they would look jealously upon the silver cup assessing its value and assuming he had stolen it from one of their friends. He was tempted to cower like a whipped puppy and run away from their angry glare with his tail between his legs.

The hungry ones looked to him with begging eyes. Their starving faces and outstretched hands told him that he held the key to their prison of hunger. Inwardly he felt that he

Life with God

was somehow responsible for their condition. Their pleading eyes followed him as he walked. Often one of them would fix his gaze on the silver cup swinging from his belt and lick his parched lips anticipating a cool drink.

The indifferent people did not acknowledge his presence. Even when they stumbled into him by accident they gave no indication of it. They were intently preoccupied rummaging through the garbage of the fat ones for some morsel of food or other valuable item that could be traded for food.

The young man was saddened by the disturbing condition of the desperate people. He wanted to flee to the familiar security of his home with the elders. But the town surrounded him in all directions and he did not know the way out. He felt in his heart he should offer help. If only to the thirsty people.

He untied the silver cup from his belt and offered it to one of the thirsty ones. As he did, several more of them immediately surrounded him. The one who reached the cup first grabbed it violently from the young man. He then put it to his lips and tipped his head back to drink from it. Realizing the cup was empty he threw it to the ground in disgust. Staring hopelessly at the empty cup, the others backed away from the young man.

As the crowd dispersed, one of the fat ones walked over quickly and kicked at two of the indifferent ones who had run to grab the discarded cup. He slurred an obscenity at the two he had kicked and bent down with a labored groan and picked up the cup. He straightened up gasping to catch his breath. He then studied the cup. It was obvious to the young man that he admired the silver cup. For a moment the young man thought the fat one intended to keep the cup. Instead, he just laughed mockingly, as saliva dripped from his lips, and

The Silver Cup

pulled out of his coat pocket a much larger cup. It did not shine like the silver cup because it was tarnished with years of dirt and grime. There was but one shiny place on the fat one's cup. That was the place where his plump pink lips frequently sucked rich, intoxicating liquids from the edge of the rim. He handed the silver cup back to the young man and wiped drool from his large lips with the arm of his grease stained coat. Then he grunted, turned, and waddled away laughing. Many of the other fat ones laughed with him and raised their large cups in a salute to their fat friend.

The young man tied the silver cup back to his belt. He felt hopeless and helpless. He turned from the scene and sadly began searching for a way out of the town. As he did a strange fog began to seep in through the streets of the town. It swirled and flowed like a low cloud slowly covering the street. By the time it reached the young man it had become waist deep. He could no longer see his feet or the street. He was amazed by the encroaching fog but was not fearful of it. It swirled up around him until he was totally engulfed in it. He could see nothing.

In a moment the fog began to dissipate. It began at his head and slowly worked its way toward his feet. As soon as he could see he realized to his amazement that he was no longer standing in the street of the town of the followers of other gods. He was standing in a pasture of rolling green hills. The grass was thick and soft. The air was crisp and fresh. As he breathed in deeply he felt energized by the air. It felt as though his body and mind were drawing nourishment from the air.

Then a man spoke to him. "Hello, young man, and welcome." He turned around and saw a man much older than he smiling pleasantly at him.

"Hello," the young man replied.

The man spoke again with kindness; "You've had some questions, haven't you?"

"Why, uh yes, I have quite a few," he answered.

"Which one would you like to start with?" the man asked.

Without hesitating, the young man blurted out, "Is the God of the elders real?"

"Yes, of course," came the immediate reply.

"Then why does He not speak with them anymore?" the young man asked.

"Because they have no desire to listen." The answer was short but not unkind.

"Why?" the young man asked emphatically.

"Because they are satisfied. But you are not, are you?"

"No" the young man said quickly, "I'm not satisfied. And I'm becoming a bit fearful that God does not exist. If He did, wouldn't He want to speak with me? If He is who the elders say he is, I think He would speak to me."

"He has been speaking to you, young man. And you have been listening. He is pleased with your efforts and your questions. I have come to explain to you what He desires of you. Will you listen?"

"Yes, of course," the young man agreed quickly.

"Yes, I believe you will listen. But, will you also do what He asks? Many desire to know His will but few desire to do His will. This is where many of His followers stumble. You see, there is very little difficulty knowing His will. Remember, the elders read from the book and His will is made plain. But when it comes to actually doing His will, many fall terribly short of His best for them. They see it as just too difficult, when really doing His will is merely inconvenient. It means they will need to change their priorities. They don't like doing that. They will do almost anything except that. But, by changing one's priorities one discovers the joy of living as one of His followers."

"What!" the young man interrupted, "Are you implying the elders are not living as His followers?"

"Oh, no!" But, they are following Him because of the personal pleasure they receive from living as His followers. Those benefits are theirs as a result of merely living clean, quiet, orderly lives."

"Well what's wrong with that?" the young man asked again. "Nothing, really," the older man said calmly. "Yet, there is a much better way of life, the benefits of which they never see."

"Then I must know about this better way so I can receive the benefit," the young man said.
"You cannot know it until you make a decision to live it. Surrender is the door to this life. The benefits of your surrender however, are not yours. They belongs to others."

"What? I'm confused," the young man admitted.

"To live this better life you must surrender your self-centered outlook to embrace a God-centered one. You then become more concerned with what you do for others rather than what God does for you. His will is that you live to love others as He does. Your life no longer matters. On this higher plane your goals, your plans, your wants, your needs are all buried in your love for Him. His love then empowers you to live to serve others, instead of serving yourself. Thus, they benefit from your sacrifice."

"But how can I live for others? It seems so difficult?" he asked.

"How?" is not the issue," the older man said with conviction in his voice. "For this is not something you can do in your own strength. Make no mistake about it, unless He supplies you with the power to live for others, it cannot be done. So, the real question is not "How" but "When?"

"When?" the young man asked.

"Yes, when do you want to get started?" the older man responded sincerely.

The young man began to feel anxious. The older man was speaking on a difficult topic. He was being asked to surrender his goals and plans so that he could be empowered to live for the benefit of others. He was frightened and unsure of what he was committing himself to.

The older man spoke again. "A moment ago you were excited. Now, you seem hesitant? Is there something troubling you?"

"Yes, well, I was considering all that I might give up in order to serve others," the young man said self-consciously. Then he added, "I'm not sure I can do it."

The Silver Cup

"Come with me," the older man said, and he turned to walk toward a stream a short distance from where they stood. The younger man followed obediently.

Reaching the stream, the older man turned and asked, "May I have your cup?"

The young man untied it from his belt and handed it to the older man.

The old man then dipped it into the stream. "Here, drink from it." He offered the young man the cup.

The young man tipped the silver cup to his mouth and drank some of the cool refreshing water.

"Oh, my!" he exclaimed after he swallowed the water. "This is delicious." He turned the cup up again and drained it. "Oh, what delicious water this is!" He had never tasted anything so satisfying.

The older man smiled knowingly. "There is no water as refreshing. You see, you have tasted the love of God. It is the water from this stream that empowers you to live for others."

"May I have more?" the young man asked.
"You may have as much as you desire," the man answered. The young man dropped to his knees to refill the cup.

While he drank, the older man continued to explain. "There is no end to His love. God desires that you drink from this stream often. To drink from it though, you must first surrender the concerns for your personal life. Then come and drink, and when you have filled your cup, take it to the ones who are thirsty like yourself. But use caution. Do not offer the thirsty ones a drink from an empty cup. Many of the elders before you have done much harm by such practice. Their motive was compassionate but their cup was empty. They speak the words of God by faithfully telling His story. But, the primary purpose of His story is to inspire them to live the better life. They have lost sight of that purpose. That is why they do not succeed in their negotiations to end the feud with the followers of the other gods. You see, for them, the cup is more important than its contents. Yet, God designed the cup for carrying the water of His love to the thirsty."

IV

The young man awoke slowly from his dream. The sun was shining down through the treetops, the river sang its murmuring song, and the young man was finally at peace. He stood up and stretched. He noticed his thirst was gone. He felt satisfied and refreshed. He bent down to pick up the silver cup. But it was not where he had placed it! He looked around him in every direction, even in the water near the rock, thinking he may have knocked it off the rock while he slept. But the cup was not there. Then he heard the older man's gentle voice again.

"Go now, take the refreshing water of my love to the thirsty. But don't make the mistake the elders have made. Remember to return often. For, just as the cup is useless without the water, so you are useless without my love."

The young man climbed down from the rock. He knew what he must do. He knew his part in ending the feud was to live among the thirsty ones in the town of the followers of other gods. With joy and peace in his heart, he set off for the town.

The End

Further Understanding of Life With God

God said through the writer of the letter to the Hebrews, 11:6; "And without faith it impossible to please God, because anyone who comes to Him must believe that He exists, and that He rewards those who earnestly seek Him." This scripture presents us with the most basic element of our life with God. That is; to enjoy the benefits of life with God, we must believe He exists. It sounds ridiculous to most Christians. "Of course we believe in God. We accepted Jesus as our Savior and Lord years ago. Why of course we believe God exists!" But do you really? I believe if we pause for a moment and look closer at this scripture we may receive a little more revelation regarding the condition of our relationship with God.

Hebrews 11:6 implies, as does all scripture, that we must know God the way He wants to be known. We cannot say we know God because we have accepted Jesus as Lord any more than we can say we know the president of the United States because we voted for him! In this passage and in many others the word, know, means to possess intimate knowledge of someone or something. In this case, that someone is God. God wants us to have more than information of Him. He wants us to have a relationship with Him that is compatible with His desires. Jesus addresses the subject of right relationship as well. To those who had done miracles in Jesus' name and addressed Him as Lord, Jesus said, in Matthew 7:23, "Then I will tell them plainly, I never knew you. Away from me, you evildoers!" What? They did miracles in His name? And He did not know them? Yes, it's sad but true. They were running around doing what they thought was pleasing to God and doing it with His power, but they did not have an intimate relationship with Him!

The point is that we must know God the way He wants us to know Him. He wants us to know Him as a child knows his parents. However, in our culture too many children do not even know their parents. It is possible then for them to think they know God even though, from God's perspective, they really do not. Jesus wants to be known by us as a husband knows his wife. But we all know the deplorable condition of most marriages. It's true. Children do not know their parents, any more than husbands know their wives. To be intimate with God is to love Him and to be loved by Him. The sad truth is many people alive today have never experienced an intimate relationship with anyone, much less with God. It is sad that our culture has promoted the erroneous belief that a sexual relationship is an intimate relationship. This idea confuses love with sex! Yet, anyone who has known true love knows a loving relationship is much more than sex. Dogs have sex. Yet, we would never think they have a loving relationship? Simply put, to know God is to love Him.

When God speaks of knowing Him He means we must know Him to be who He says He is! We must encounter Him in our daily lives. We must see and feel and be touched by His loving power. He wants us to be touched by it in practical ways. Hebrews 6:11 implies that we must know Him by believing, seeing, and receiving the rewards of that knowledge! This is much different than knowing about Him. We can know about Him by reading about Him. We can read the Bible to learn about God. However, our reading should reveal the depths of God's love for us, and thus inspire us to pursue a deeper relationship with God. That's why He wrote it! If our Bible study does not draw us closer to God, I wonder if it has any value at all!

God gave us the written Word so we could understand Him and discover His unfailing love for us. Reading about His interaction with men who lived before us shows, time after time, His love. Throughout the Bible, from cover to cover, story after story, chapter after chapter, we see God's interaction with man. The Bible reveals to us an epic true story of God's constant pursuit of a relationship with man and man's constant rejection of God. Next time you read it, read it from that perspective and you will see what I mean.

God designed man to have fellowship with God. Man was to be God's friend. One could go so far as to say man was to be God's best friend! Looking at the endless variety of life in the universe, from jellyfish to planets, one can easily see the range and depth of God's infinite creativity. Yet, isn't it interesting to note that man is the only created thing that is made in the image and likeness of God. In our passage from Hebrews scripture states Enoch was taken from the earth before he died. This happened to show that it was possible for man to have that much faith in God! God rewarded Enoch for his faithfulness to God by taking Him home before he died of natural causes! What a wonderful testimony of God's desire to know man and to be known by him.

To know God properly, we must know Him as He wishes to be known. That is, intimately. As we pursue our relationship by meeting with Him, sitting and talking quietly with Him, He will reveal Himself to us. He promises this throughout scripture. It may feel strange at first. It may be difficult to develop a consistent time and place to meet with

God. But it is not impossible and it is so desirable! Our God, who loves us, will help in the process.

God is always looking for man. He is always seeking to meet with man. Consider these statements from the Bible; "Adam where are you?" "Come, let us reason," "For I know the plans I have for you," "Be strong and courageous. Do not be terrified. Do not be discouraged, for the Lord your God will be with you, wherever you go." "Come to me you who are weary," "I will never leave you or forsake you," "Behold, I stand at the door and knock." These statements were made by God, the creator and sustainer of the universe! The faith He desires us to possess is the faith that says, "I know God is with me, I know He is for me, I know He is my provider, I know He is my healer, I know He is my savior, I know He is my ever present help in times of trouble, and I know He rewards me for my friendship with Him. I know all of this because I know God."

This is God, the One who calls us to Himself. He is not like our parents, our siblings, our children, our pastor, our employer. This is God. The Eternal One who never leaves us, never forsakes us. This is our loving heavenly Father, the One who designed us, and created us to have relationship with Him. He desires to have us in His presence more than we desire to be in His presence! As we begin to pursue Him as He has always pursued us, we will begin to see Him more and more as He truly is. Doing so will make us hungry for more of Him. We will desire Him more than we desire anything else. When we taste and see the Lord, He is good, He truly will become our all in all.

Are you getting hungry? God is here and He is waiting to meet with you. What else could be more important? In Matthew 6:21, Jesus, speaking to the multitudes said this, "For where your treasure is, there your heart will be also."

This life will end very soon. Ninety or so years may seem like a long time. Yet, too many people do not live nearly that long. But in terms of the endless eons of eternity ninety years is no longer than the amount of time it takes to read this sentence. Jesus assures us if we make time with God our highest priority, all the trouble of this temporary life on Earth will be seen from a more realistic perspective; that is God's perspective. Life with God does not guarantee smooth sailing. But as difficult as this life can sometimes be; there will peace. I encourage you to pick up your Bible and read Matthew 6:25-34 again.

Prayer

Mike Green, 1995

There is a place
Amid gravity's grip
To delight both the eye and heart.
So often lost
Within the stress
Life on earth imparts.
Oh, how it glows
with radiant light
As I persevere in prayer.
Sweet joy is mine
As we embrace
Such peace engulfs me there.

Then loosed from earth
And all these trials
To soar celestial waves.
The dread of living
Among this grief
Removed by Christ who saves.
Oh, glorious
Eternal life,
How can this goodness be?
Such holy love,
My God in Christ,
Your grace has rescued me!

Should I resist
This wondrous place
I'm tied by life to earth.
And reject the call
That would take me where
There is no pain of birth.
Yet when I pause
With faith and hope
Against earth's tide so strong,
With love He speaks
And I'm assured
'Tis there that I belong.

Dear friend, it is our sincere prayer that you will pursue God through a deeply personal relationship. He wants you to have life with Him. He wants to make Himself known to you. He calls you and He awaits your reply. Run to Him today! Sit with Him, and let Him pour His love over you. He is faithful.

Introducing
Mike and Michele Green

For the past 23 years, Mike and Michele Green, founders and directors of Bless God Ministries, have worked as a team offering Bible based counseling services to people from around the world. Mike and Michele celebrated their thirty-first wedding anniversary in 2007. After studying and practicing occult religions for 20 years, they submitted to the Lordship of Jesus Christ in early 1984. Their fascinating testimony was filmed by and shown on "The 700 Club."

Mike earned his Master's Degree in Family Counseling from Regent University in Virginia Beach, Virginia. He also holds a Bachelor's Degree in Theology.

Mike and Michele are licensed and ordained by *The Healing House Network*, an international network of counseling ministers. Currently, they train RTF ministers at the *Restoring the Foundations International Training Center* in Hendersonville, North Carolina. They also travel extensively within the network and at this time have invitations to teach in seven different countries around the world.

Life with God

Through their fourteen-year association with *Restoring The Foundations Ministry* and *The Healing House Network*, Mike and Michele have counseled hundreds of people averaging 1,800 session hours per year. People have come from cities and towns all over the USA from Maine to Washington, and from Florida to California. Some have traveled from as far away as Canada, Alaska, England, Holland, Denmark, Singapore, Sri Lanka, South Africa, China, Japan, Hawaii, and Mexico to receive counsel from Mike and Michele.

In addition to their role as teachers, Mike and Michele enjoy a healthy pastoral relationship with several individuals and couples in the states and in other countries. Always encouraging and affirming, Mike and Michele have a passion to help all of God's children believe the incredible truth, "You are a member of the Royal Family and God your Father, the King of the Universe, loves you unconditionally and eternally. He has a wonderful plan for your life which includes fulfilling every promise He has made."

Mike and Michele have published two books so far, with several more in various stages of the writing process. *Effective Listening,* published in 1998, is a counseling handbook focused on helping new counselors develop listening skills. *Life With God* is the incredible true story of their walk with God. Mike has also written and published a music CD, *Jesus, My Healer.*

Bless God Ministries
Know Christ | Love God | Serve Man

102 Mohegan Rd
St. Augustine, Florida 32086
904-794-5877
mnmgreen@gmail.com

www.ingramcontent.com/pod-product-compliance
Lightning Source LLC
Chambersburg PA
CBHW020001050426
42450CB00005B/275